What I Meant to Say Was...

Carl — Thank you for your service — for putting your life on the line every day! It was great to meet you and Mark!

Hoping you enjoy my stories!

Bill Kolwaite
7-29-19

What I Meant to Say Was...

Nearly drowning, a man is given the opportunity to revisit his past, learning how it can help him and others.

BILL KOLOVANI

WHAT I MEANT TO SAY WAS...
*Nearly drowning, a man is given the
opportunity to revisit his past, learning
how it can help him and others.*

Copyright © 2018 Bill Kolovani

All rights reserved

Published by:
Tremendous Leadership
PO Box 267
Boiling Springs, PA 17007

717-701-8159   800-233-2665

www.TremendousLeadership.com

ISBN: 978-1-949033-07-6

Printed in the United States of America.

TABLE OF CONTENTS

PREFACE

Being a first-generation American baby boomer, I wanted to share my story. As a teenager, my father came to America as a stow-away on a Greek Freighter fleeing his native country of Albania after falsely being accused of murder. Me, I was the last of six children, a true surprise after my father had established his family of five. I flunked eighth grade, and then I became a high school dropout. However, as you will read in my story, when persistence overcomes resistance anything can happen!

Everyone has their personal story. Some people's stories may appear to be pretty mundane, while other stories are near unbelievable and one wonders how the person lived to tell their tale! Others have been blessed to have an interesting life, wide and varied like the fictional television commercial character of Jonathan Goldsmith. You might know him from the Mexican *Dos Equis* beer commercials as "The most interesting man in the world." The experiences in my life have frequently left me feeling blessed, privileged, desperate, and sometimes cursed, and sometimes these feelings were all evident in the same situation.

No, I wasn't fortunate enough to be born of royalty, wealth or with the proverbial "silver spoon in my mouth," but I have been fortunate in many other ways. Mainly, I have been blessed with having a personal relationship with Jesus Christ. Beyond being blessed in this way, I was gifted with two incredible daughters and three granddaughters. But, along the way, I managed to keep touching the hot stove and burning myself over and over again. I use this as a metaphor to describe my life of sin. Even today, I still wonder how I could have continued to make the same stupid mistakes over and over again. With God's grace, I was fortunate to make it to the other side and survive.

I have heard it said about me more than once, that my life is like that of a cat with nine lives. I seem to always have landed on my feet time and time again after failure—just like a cat with its built-in twisting reaction to constantly land upright. Oh, sometimes it would take a little longer to get back on my feet, but eventually God would motivate me and give me another ride of my life! I had a knack to make things work no matter how little experience or knowledge I had going in. I'm sure it was a God thing!

Along the way I gained a lot of knowledge from my mistakes. I wanted to share these experiences—whether they were good or bad—hoping they'll be able to help others in their journey through life.

Maybe, you can relate to one or more of my exploits and learn that bad decisions, false beliefs, or failures do not necessarily bring forth "the end of the world," but there are consequences.

We may fail, but if you learn from the failure, resolve to do better the next time, and grab your bootstraps and try again—with God's help you can regain your footing and have a life of success.

Hopefully, as you read about my life's journey it will bring hope and the knowledge that no matter how many times you fail, God is there to pick you up, help you start over, and become the success you were meant to be.

Bill Kolovani

Chapter 1

A BEAUTIFUL DAY FOR GOLF

It's an incredibly beautiful day, so I decided to go golfing. Lately, I've been having trouble with my asthma, but according to the locals, it's just the allergy season and it will get better as soon as the pollen is over.

Although my breathing is tight occasionally, which makes me think about my health and early warning signs of a heart attack. I have never had a heart attack and I have good communication with my body. I know my health and how to take care of it. I'm not susceptible to any health-related problems, especially today, while I am doing something as relaxing as golfing.

I'm doing something today that I don't usually do—I'm walking the golf course. I didn't do cardio today when I worked out at the local fitness center, so I figured the walk would do me good. The attendant at the golf course fixed me up with a motorized push cart, loaded up my golf clubs, and I was off. It's a glorious late spring day here as most spring days are. The sky is cloudless, no humidity, a very light breeze, and the temperature is in the low 70s. It's one of those perfect days that everyone dreams about.

I'm a casual cigar smoker, but today I thought, "I will not smoke while golfing. After all, I'm walking and getting some extra cardio exercise, and I certainly would never smoke a cigar at the gym." I approach the number one hole. I see that it's a 119-yard par three downhill hole with an uphill elevated green. It's surrounded by lots of sand traps, and a pin location that funnels your ball right to the bunker. Your tee shot has to be hit straight; otherwise, you're in trouble to the right from dense thorn bushes or to the left the 9th fairway. I hit a perfect tee shot just short of the pin. My ball had a slight backspin, it checked up and rolled only slightly past the pin by about eight feet. This enabled me to par the first hole, and I putted in, in two strokes for a three. I was feeling great. I hadn't parred that hole all year long. I was a little winded, and my heart was slightly racing a bit. But, I just figured it was the walk down and uphill and lugging my bag full of 17 clubs, six dozen balls, and enough gadgets to make even the worst golfer think he could be better. I thought, "I should probably schedule a good yard sale sometime soon to get rid of some of the junk I never use," making a mental note to myself. I have a real problem —no matter how many golf balls I have in my bag—there's always room for more. Kind of like dessert— there's always room for Jell-O! So, when I have an opportunity to poke around in the rough, the pond, or a creek for someone's lost ball, I always take that opportunity to add to my obsession. After all, you can never have too many golf balls!

Holes number two and three are back to back par fours, although both holes are modest in length. There is always plenty of room for trouble, which is just about any shot for my usual game. But it seems like this day is unusual. Something feels different when I escaped difficulty on both holes with a par on two and a stupid three-putt on three for a bogey... but, hey I'm only one stroke over after three holes! Now I'm feeling like—Bill Murray called him—"Your Eminence," the Lutheran Bishop who couldn't miss a shot in the movie *Caddyshack*.

The fourth hole is a long 504-yard par five. This par five is long and strong; downhill from the tee box to a generous landing area about 100 yards long and then it proceeds slightly uphill towards the green to the left. I hit a beautiful tee shot with a slight left to right fade (I used to have an awful slice) landing 260 yards right center of the fairway, giving me a beautiful wide-open shot to the green. I choose my three-wood, but I know I can never get there from here with this club or with any other club I have in my bag.

I'm once again noticing this strange feeling of my heart palpitating uncontrollably, almost creating a nervous sense like that of a first kiss. But I shrug it off, thinking it's just the hard walk. I hit my three-wood on the screws, dead center with the correct hinge of the wrists sucking all the power humanly possible from the club and pounding it up the fairway. The fairway grass was short allowing the ball to roll, and roll, landing the ball strangely enough right in front of the putting green several feet into the first cut. I've played this hole a lot. I've had lots of sevens, a few eights, and too many out-of-bounds to care to score and more three putts than Judge Smails. But here I am laying two just off the green in the middle of a deep approaching fringe.

Sizing up the situation, I ponder, "Shall I use The Texas Wedge (my putter) or try my pitching wedge?" I decide that I have more control with my putter. I look at the hole facing the cup; then walk all the way around the back side of the green facing the flag, eyeing my ball location. I've never had an eagle, and

I can count the birdies on my two hands. I am a 22 handicap, and I can play to a 30 at any given moment in time. I walk back to my ball thinking, "Who's going to believe me if I sink this putt anyway? I have no witness! It's my word against no one—just me and the score-card." I kneel to eye the putt once again. I stand over the putt like it's for the Master's Championship, looking at the left to right angulation, thinking about the ball marks, scuffs on the greens from previous heavy shoed golfers, and so on. I take one final look and address my old scuffed found ball. Thoughts race through my mind... "It's a long putt, don't go past the hole, don't leave it short, don't push it, and don't drag your putter before hitting the ball. I'm overthinking—just putt the ball, stupid!"

I focus once again on the hole. Starting from several feet outside the fringe, I glance down at my putter and line it face-up with my target spot and stroke the ball hard for my 40-plus foot putt. I pull my putter back and strike the ball firm sending it sailing towards the angulation. Off to the left the ball goes, turning slightly as it heads downhill, and then follows the landscape to the right, making its way to the right side of the cup, bending towards the cup, and stopping less than a foot from the hole. "Wow!" I say out loud. As I take a breath, my heart is ready to pop out of my chest. I walk up to the ball. Normally, I would just knock it into the hole or take a gimme, but I think, "Hey it's for a birdie." I've never birdied this hole in my entire life, and frankly, I'm not sure that I've parred this hole that many times. I line it up—almost shaking at the knees. I pull my putter back slightly and bump the ball sending it in motion. I rim the cup using the entire circumference as my ball three-sixties around it before it drops to the bottom for a birdie!

As I bend down to pick my ball out of the hole, I reach for it, and I feel like I pulled something in the left side of my chest. But I shake it off thinking, "Hey, when I did my exercise this morning I worked my chest, my shoulders, and my pectorals—it's just soreness or stiffness from working my body physically this morning at the gym." I scored my birdie and I am now even par after four holes of golf. The weather is sensational, and I've been able to remove myself from all the tension that life has been dealing me lately.

I have been tremendously blessed over the years—traveling the world over, enjoying good wine, and smoking fine cigars. To say the least, I've been blessed being able to afford most things that many people just never get to experience! But the last five or six years of my life have been filled with tremendous hurt including the dissolving of a 28-year marriage in an ugly divorce. When I think about it, is there any divorce that is really pretty? If that's not enough, I closed my advertising agency after nearly 25 years and sold off my commercial real-estate holdings losing over 10 million dollars in the liquidation of assets. All that being said, none of my past pressures crept into my life today. It was just me, the fresh, clean air, and my game of golf... which I love!

Unlike yesterday, today my golf game is dead on. I park my pull cart at the bottom of the steps of the fifth hole. The hole is playing about 129 yards today, so I grab my nine iron, and my lucky tee, and climb the 15 or so steps up the hill to the tee box. This is another beautiful hole, but a testy little par three with an out-of-bounds, tree-lined, right side. You have to aim your tee shot to the green between the flag and the bunker on the right side of the postage sized green to avoid hitting the gigantic oak tree branches that overhang on the left side of the green. If you hit a slight hook shot—that's the perfect shot—pulling you in from the right, you'll avoid trouble from the towering tree on the left. But I tend to slice the ball more often than not; I need to have virtually pin-point accuracy to reach the green safely—if I am going to keep my streak of even par alive. To make matters worse, there is a meandering stream that surrounds two-thirds of the green, fringe, and bunker area on this hole.

Still feeling a bit short of breath, a little light-headed, and now feeling a sense of fullness or squeezing pain in the center of my chest—I eye the hole from behind the tee box. Wow, I can really feel the cigars from the many rounds before and they're kicking my butt. Tee and ball in my right hand, I bend down and place my ball on my lucky tee, and slide the tee into the soft turf. I stand up and step back once again looking for a target to make sure my ball and stance are lined up correctly. I pause for a minute or two enjoying the lushness of the view, taking a few deep breaths, hoping this strange feeling in my chest will subside soon.

I grab my club with my sweaty hands and place them on the grip of my club. Rolling my hands around it several times, hoping to dry the moisture off of them that they're suddenly producing. I'm standing over the ball, positioning my alignment to my target, lining up the face of the club to my target spot as well. I step away from the ball, holding my nine iron in my left hand, removing my hat with my right hand, wiping the sweat from my forehead with my forearm. I place my hat back on my head moving it around several times soaking up the sweat. I grip my club once again with both hands, aligning myself to my target—just a solid nine iron away. I waggle my club and realign, glancing at the flag, eyeing my destination, and look back down at my ball. I pull my club back on my backswing with a feeling of confidence and control—a nice fluid motion. As I reach the top of my backswing and start my downward swing towards the ball, I come through with a slight bit of hesitation causing me to chunk my shot taking a huge divot. It's a high straight shot towards the green, but it's going to be way short of it. The ball may have traveled 90-plus yards and *sploosh*, my ball finds its way into the creek!

Chapter 2

THE RIVER OF DREAMS!

I guess it was bound to happen sooner or later—I was so hoping my 22 handicap wouldn't rear its ugly head. I walked down the steps to my pull cart, slammed my nine-iron into the bag, and headed towards the fifth green. Feeling some frustration as I was walking, I soon remembered what Walter Hagen said, "Two bad shots and one good shot and you're right back in the hole!" So, I'm only laying one, but who knows where? With a good shot from the edge of the creek bed, I could be on the green and right back in the hole again with possibly a par or maybe just a bogey!

I felt winded heading down the pathway towards the fifth green and crossing the small bridge that leads over the creek. As I crossed the bridge, I start to glance to the right looking around for something white; hoping my golf ball will appear around the creek bed or marsh grass at what I thought was my landing spot and point of entry for my shot. I noticed it implanted in the mud at the foot of a four-foot embankment of dark brown, fertile soil; too far down the bank to stand on top of the bank and get a swing at the ball. So, I will have to lower myself to the creek and try to plow it out of there or take a penalty stroke. As I get closer and stand over the ball staring at it from the thick grassy topside of the bank, I see that I definitely need to crawl down the bank to the creek to attempt to hit my ball. I also notice the bank curls around towards the top from the bank erosion. So, if I can hit the ball with my sand wedge, chances are I can't get it up high enough without it ricocheting back towards the other side of the creek.

I grab my sand wedge and start to pull it from my bag as I feel this strange feeling moving down my arm. I manage to get my club out of the bag. I drop to one knee with excruciating chest pain, all the while trying to use my golf club as a cane or prop to hold myself up and keep from falling into the creek. I have no strength, I'm seeing stars, and feeling very light headed as I fall down into the creek, deep into the marsh grass, head first.

I feel this coolness all over me, engulfing my entire body, but no strength is available to do anything about my position in the cool waters of the creek bed as I fall into a partial unconscious state. My world is spinning around and around with what seems like my life passing before my eyes. I have no idea where I am.

It's dark and cool. "Where am I? What's going on with me?", thoughts pass through my mind. I'm totally blacked out. People are flashing before my eyes, like one of those psychedelic light shows from the 1970s. There are people that I recognize and others that I have never seen or met before in my life.

I get a flashback of falling into the creek. I can almost see myself lying in the grassy marsh and then my mind goes completely dark again. In this unconscious state, I get a burst of energy. I try to lift my head up to see where I'm at and how I can get out of my predicament—but I have another rush of chest pain, followed by a flash of light. I have no movement in my body; I can't pull myself up out of the water and the marsh. Battling back and forth in my mind, I can feel water rushing into my mouth, around my cheeks and face, my nose, and my left ear.

It's dark, and I have the thought, "Is this what my life finally comes down to? If so, God, go ahead and bring me home! I've been running on fumes for many years now; how long am I supposed to do this? I can't go on any longer. I have lost everything financially—a divorce and more!" I continue to view my world spinning around me; I'm able to see 20, 30, and even 40 years of my life quickly flashing before me.

I hear a voice, but I have no idea where it is coming from. I can't lift my head to see anyone talking to me. "You're not alone, even my choice servants have felt the same way—Moses, Elijah, and even Jeremiah! I know your condition; I know you are frustrated right now with life not knowing where your future is headed, but I know your plans! Why don't you rest for a while, go to sleep, and just rest; rest my child."

I cry out to God, "Save me, O God, for the floodwaters are up to my neck. Deeper and deeper I sink into the mire; I can't find a foothold. I am in deep water, and the floods overwhelm me. I am exhausted from crying for help; my throat is parched. My eyes are swollen with weeping, waiting for my God to help me. Lord, save me and remove me from the pain that I have experienced with the loss of my businesses, with my bankruptcy, and my divorce; I can't stand this pain any longer! My heart pounds in my chest. The terror of death assaults me. Fear and trembling overwhelm me, and I can't stop shaking. Oh, that I had wings like a dove, then I would fly away and rest! O Lord, how long will you forget me—forever? How long will you look the other way? How long must I struggle with anguish in my soul, with sorrow in my heart? Will this continue every day? How long will my enemy have the upper hand over me?"

I'm awakened; I can see a light, and it is getting brighter. Sunlight is glaring in my face. It looks like I'm in a cave. My surroundings are serene and dim. I can see what looks like an opening... to wherever I ended up. I find myself able to get up from a sitting position and am now standing against what I think is the wall of a cave. Questions flow through my mind, "Am I at the entrance of a cave? (I shuffle my feet not wanting to trip and fall because I don't have any shoes on.) Where are my shoes? This is very strange! Where am I?" I can clearly see an opening as my eyes rapidly adjust to the dimly lit area that I'm in. I can see an opening of the rocks to what appears to be just 30 or 40 feet away. I walk towards the light of the opening, carefully taking each step, shuffling my feet as I go. The closer I get to the opening and the light I can see more clearly... I now know for certain that I am in a cave. Questions come to mind again, "What am I doing here? How in the world did I get here?" I manage to get to the opening, and I walk outside of a mountain made of huge, smooth rocks. My eyes are squinting to adjust to the light. "Where am I?" I whisper out loud. I hear water rushing from a nearby stream or river; the sun is bright—brightly shining in my face. I have never been here before, and I don't recognize anything about this area. There are no cars, no roads, no signs of life; just a pathway leading away from the cave entrance to a river, and a sign that reads, "The River of Dreams!" There is an open area like that of the Grand Canyon, but I still don't recognize any of my surroundings. The beauty was breathtaking, "Oh, God, how beautiful is your creation!", resonated loudly throughout my whole being.

As I'm walking away from the cave, I look back at the Herculean mountain that I came out of. I turn back around and start walking to where—I have no idea—but I feel led to move on, to walk to the edge of the water, and to the "River of Dreams!"

I get a flashback of my golf game, but I have no idea what it means. I get another flashback of the pain in my chest, and as I get the flashback I grab my chest, and I feel no pain, whatsoever. I breathe deeply; there is no pain, no shortness of breath. Again, thoughts race through my mind, "Did I die? Did I drown when I fell into the creek? Did I have a heart attack and die? Did I die and am I about to meet my Creator? If I am dead, I sure feel pretty healthy." I pinch my skin, I touch my face, I run my hands over my head—I have a full head of hair again! I rub my arms. I feel incredible like I'm youthful again. The skin on my body is tight. My hands have no wrinkles—what is going on here?

The pathway is dusty made from red soil. It would lead you to believe the river was once broader and more ferocious than it is today. I can feel the warm air on my face. It's sunny, it's very comfortable, there's a light breeze with no humidity, and it is so incredibly picturesque! The pathway moves around the pillaring red and brown rocks and cliffs, creating some shade from the river banks. I have no idea where I am to go. I'm feeling tired all of a sudden. I have no energy at all. I sit down for a short rest on one of the rocks that's protected from the sun. Leaning up against another rock with my back, enjoying the beauty of all that's around me, I immediately dozed off.

Chapter 3

ALWAYS TAKE THE INITIATIVE

I'm gently awakened by the soft touch of my mother. I'm sitting beside her, alert and now in a different place and setting altogether. I'm in the living room of our house where I lived as a child. I'm four, or not quite five-years-old, yet I know I'm able to think like an adult from someplace in my distant past. It's strange, very strange, almost like a Rod Sterling episode of *The Twilight Zone!*

I am sitting on our old gray "pleather"—plastic, or leather couch—I was never sure what kind of sofa it was. My mother is rubbing my cold feet to warm them as she puts on my socks. She pulls my socks up over my calves, all the while massaging my small feet with such kindness and compassion. We are watching our round screened black and white console television and the afternoon soap operas are on. I remembered I hated those things, *As the World Turns* and others. My mother would often fold the laundry, do the ironing, and watch TV to pass the time until my brothers and sisters would arrive home from school for dinner. But, she would always take time out for me to make me feel special. Mom was kind and giving to everyone without exception. If she had two dollars and someone needed a dollar, she would gladly give that person both of them, so they had more than she did.

When I think about it, there were so many things I wish I would have said to my mother before she passed away. She was the most encouraging person I have ever met. She could make me believe I could accomplish anything, and frankly, through her encouragement, I did achieve many beautiful things later in my life! She always stressed, "Take the initiative," "do something," and "put your best effort into whatever you do." She made me believe you can do anything you set your mind to.

Over the years, I learned that the mind is in the "Spiritual Realm," where Satan has access because he is in the Spiritual Realm. You need to train your mind to be disciplined with discernment, and most of all, meditation. As a man thinks in his heart, so he does! Your mind is power; allow God in and renew your thoughts, your mind, and your spirit. She might not have said it this way as I was growing up, but that's how I interpreted it as years went on.

So now I told her what I wish I would have always talked to her about—what I always meant to say. When I dropped out of school in eleventh grade, or for that fact, when I flunked eighth grade, these were two of the things I needed to get off my chest with her! I was the youngest of six children, and mom always gave in to me and allowed me to have my own way. I blurted out, "Mom, you are too easy on me!" Perhaps my mother indulged me because I had asthma. Maybe she coddled me because I was so sickly and had so many brushes with death throughout my life. And maybe she enabled me because I was the baby of the family. Her reply was simple, "We are not God, and we cannot do what

God will do. But, if you take the initiative and put all your effort into whatever you are doing, God will see you through your task at hand. God will not give us good habits or character, and at the same time, He will not force us to walk correctly; we have to do those things ourselves. We must get into the habit of doing things, and doing things right, take the initiative to start at the beginning!" And then she asked me, "How do you eat an elephant? One bite at a time." I never knew where that quote came from, but the metaphor was always easy enough to understand, and I never forgot her saying that when things looked too tough to handle.

I came along late in life for my parents. My mother was 39-years-old, and my dad was 51-years-old when I was born. Let's face it, they were both worn out. Five other kids had sucked the life out of them before I came onto the scene. I was the surprise child. There was a six-year gap between my youngest sister and myself. When I was just 13-years-old, and in the seventh grade, my father died. I think these were all critical issues to my mother making me feel like her favorite. Whether I was her favorite or not, frankly, I think, she made each one of the kids feel like they were the most special child in her life!

When I was in eighth grade, and I have to tell you, I absolutely hated school. There was never anything I really liked about school. Oh, you must understand, I enjoyed sports as most every kid does. I loved gym class, and I loved music class. I especially craved springtime in gym class when we would play softball. I could hit the ball from home plate deep into left field and bounce the ball clear onto the second story roof of the school! I'm not sure how far that was, but I know I was the only kid in school able to do that at our Junior High school.

Eighth grade was a tumultuous year for me. My mother started working a full-time job as the baker at the local hotel after my father died the spring before. She worked day and night to support the family after my dad passed away. I was left alone to come and go as I pleased and to do whatever I wanted to do with my promiscuity. My brother—with his suave and debonair ways—easily influenced me with the women in his life. He was so darn handsome. It seemed to me he always had a lovely young lady on his arm. Consequently, I wanted to be like him. So, at a ripe young age, I was filling my time being just like my idol—enjoying what I witnessed through him—filling my life with unhealthy choices!

I was pretty much left to myself, and I took full advantage of every waking mischievous moment. This, I learned later in life, was all "Negative Initiative." What I did with those moments was flirt with practically every young girl in school. (In fact, during the summer after sixth grade I discovered foreplay for the first time. I would have killed my kids for crap like that!) But as I said, eighth grade was terrible. I never studied, I could have cared less about school, and I was already into hot cars, sports, friends, and girls. I managed to fail every primary subject in school that year! Yep, you got it! Straight F's for four back-to-back marking periods in Mathematics, English, Science, and History, but I managed to get A's in health, music, and physical education.

I will never forget when grades were handed out at the end of each marking period. I had to take the report card home and show it to my mother. But, I would never show my report cards to her. I would just sign her name on it and turn it back to the teacher. The school never knew what my mother's signature looked like because I always signed her name.

Another thing I remember about that year was this: as the year came to a close—on the last day—no report card was given to me, and I was called down to see the Principal. He called me into his office, sat me down, and said, "We know you're not stupid, and we know you don't have a learning disability. We all know how you struggled losing your dad, and if you would like we will pass you on to the ninth grade." And my comment was, "No! I had F's and failing grades; I will stay behind and take the consequences of my poor performance." And so, I stayed in eighth grade the next year to prove my intelligence by, "Taking the Initiative."

In my second year of repeating the eighth grade, I made straight A's in every subject and went on to ninth grade the next year. This came to be the first thing that I really regretted about my mother. Why didn't she check on me? What was she thinking? I know she wasn't formally educated, but she had incredible natural intelligence and incredible common sense—as I learned years later. No one could pull the wool over her eyes; she could read dishonest people like an open book!

In tenth and eleventh grade, I was entirely out of control. When I turned 16, my mother bought me a brand-new Volkswagen Beetle. Oh, I would have preferred a new Corvette, but my big brother was a mechanic at the Volkswagen dealership and talked my mother into a VW. Honestly, we couldn't have afforded a new Corvette anyway. As it turns out, mom knew best, and I returned the favor and taught her at age 56 how to drive the darn thing, as well. Again, I was "Taking the Initiative." Can you imagine, a little gray-haired lady that stood about five foot nothing driving a stick shift Volkswagen? Everyone in the neighborhood thought she was cool in her little gear-shifting

V-Dub as she tooled around town, barely being able to see over the steering wheel.

I played a lot of hooky at school, I started smoking cigarettes, and I was fist fighting a lot. I have to admit, I was pretty darn good at fighting. But, as I learned years later, that was really nothing to be good at, and when someone hits you back—ouch—that hurts! In eleventh grade, I dropped out of school after being suspended for punching a guy in the nose. At one time, this same fellow had been a good friend from back in Junior High school. He was fortunate he wasn't more severely injured because I broke his nose pretty badly. When it happened, I was immediately called to the Principal's office, asked to leave, and not come back until the next year. But first, I had to bring my mother to school to sign a release for me to quit school. What I wish my mother would have said, and what I meant to speak to her during this time was: "Why are you allowing me to drop out of school?!" If that were my child, I would have grabbed them by the scruff of the neck and said to him and the Principal, "This child will be back in school on Monday, and you will give him another chance! I will be accountable for him, he will be responsible for his own actions, and he will graduate next year!" But, I persuaded my mother into allowing me to quit school and go into the work field. As it turned out, I never did graduate from high school. I had eight jobs from April that year until December finally rolled around! A year later, I did manage to get my G.E.D.

Consult the Operator's Manual
What I Meant to Say Was...

As I chatted with my mom on that old sofa that day, I told her how incredibly great she was; how much love she had for everyone, and what I meant to say! And what I meant to say was "Mom, I wish you would have been tougher on me!" She then said to me, "I knew all this was going on and happening in your life. But you were hard-headed with excellent persuasive skills and an achiever. It didn't matter what I would have said, you would have done what you wanted to anyway--you always have! I just constantly prayed for your safety in everything you did. I knew you would always land on your feet, and you always did!" She closed with, "Continue to be determined in anything you do, act immediately in the faith that God has given you, and never reconsider or change your initial decision." She continued to rub my feet as I fell asleep in her arms.

He's always there! No matter how low I've been, how far away I've strayed, how much I've cried, cast Him away, and avoided His Holy Spirit. No matter how much I've cheated, no matter how many affairs, a divorce, failures, lies, and slip-ups; He's always been there! It's like the story of the footprints in the sand... when you see just one set of footprints in the sand, God has not forsaken us. When you notice only one set of prints, that is when He's carrying us! In all of my years, He's never run from me; it's typically me running from Him!

I know He's had a vital part in my life for a long time, even before I knew Him, He knew me! One of the best things that I can say right now is "This too shall pass, and it's not going to last forever; one day soon the clouds will dissipate!" I see my answer in Philippians:

"And my God will meet all your needs according to the riches of his glory in Christ Jesus." (Philippians 4:19)

Always consult the operator's manual first! I think Mercedes Benz was the innovator of an option called "Techtronic cruise control." It's a cruise control system that actually works in conjunction with your GPS system. It has front and rear monitoring sensors to assist you in knowing you're too close for comfort. It also slows you down as you approach a car in front of you. It's about as close to autopilot as I've ever seen, of course, except for the self-driving vehicles! But my point is, it alerts you before you get into trouble. If we listen to the Holy Spirit, He'll also alert our operating systems when we're nearing trouble. God is our GPS system. He points, directs, and guides us every step of the way. All we have to do is listen to the directions He's giving us. He might be alerting you by His Word, His Holy Spirit, it could even be from someone He brings into your life, a circumstance or situation. Nevertheless, when God tugs at you, make sure you listen. You see, God is the creator of devices designed in our system to keep us from harm and trouble; all we have to do is consult the operator's manual for proper instruction!

How Can This Help You?

Forgive Yourself! Forgive and forget when something leaves an indelible mark in your life. God chose to forgive us. But He not only decides to forgive, but does not even remember our sins. God does not want to remember our sins. He chooses never to bring them up again. He doesn't forget because He cannot. But, He doesn't remember them either; that is, He will never bring them up again. Why? Because they have been forgiven in His Son Jesus!

Love and accept yourself unconditionally! God has already forgiven us, but before you can experience the wonder of unconditional love, you first have to learn to love yourself. You cannot possibly love others unconditionally before you first learn to love yourself. This is the very first step to experiencing unconditional love. Love yourself, accept yourself just as you are, and then give love to all without any expectation of it being returned—the joy is in the giving. Many people have difficulty giving love to themselves. Try this exercise: stand before a mirror, every day, and say, "I really love you... (Your name)." Keep doing this until it gets effortless and you feel happy doing it. We can now expand on this. Contact the heart energy of unconditional love and direct it to your reflection, then flood your whole body with it, and then visualize sending it out over the earth to as many others as you can.

When you read Hebrews 11, you will see a listing of great people of faith like Abraham, Moses, David, and others. None of their sins are listed, even though they were sinners. Why? Because God not only forgives sin, He chose to remember their sins no more.

One other point, Jesus told us to forgive as the Father has forgiven us. As it says in Ephesians:

"Be kind and compassionate to one another, forgiving each other, just as in Christ God forgave you." (Ephesians 4:32)

If someone does something wrong against you, and then later asks for forgiveness, and you forgive him, you are never supposed to bring up that offense again, ever! Maybe, you won't ever forget the offense, but then again, you can choose not to remember it, for me this makes it a lot easier to forgive. This is what forgiveness means for those of us who have been forgiven by Jesus. Be determined and act immediately! Never look back, once you make a decision—go with it!

"No one who puts a hand to the plow and looks back is fit for service in the kingdom of God." (Luke 9:62)

Make sure you have a great cheerleader! No matter how bad things really are in your life, make sure you have someone available to talk to that is a good encourager. It could be your best friend, an excellent golfing buddy, your spouse, or a daughter, or son. Make sure when your head is hanging low, that this person is around so they can detect it and lend the help you need. Let's face it; we all need a good quick pick-me-up every now and then. Everyone needs encouragement, especially when you are having a bad day.

Chapter 4

OUT OF THE WRECKAGE, I SURVIVED

The spring air is warm, and the bright sunshine is gently kissing my face as I find myself sitting under a maple tree, "graveside" on one of our old lawn chairs. Remember the kind of aluminum chairs with plastic woven straps? Sometimes the material was so weak, dry-rotted, and worn out, that when someone a little too heavy would sit on them, their butt would end up going right through the bottom of the chair and down they would go! Memorial Gardens Cemetery is my father's final resting place. I am 13-years-old—that's the age I was when my father passed away. I glance to my left, and my father is sitting on the lawn chair beside me. He has his typical white tee-shirt on, like the one he always wore to work at his restaurant. His arms folded across one another, smoking an unfiltered cigarette, just as I still remembered him.

I would never want to say dad was a bad father; after all, he never hit me or even scolded me—although he probably should have. But the wreckage I am referring to is the amount of time we never had together. "Pop" never spent any quality time with me during his life. I don't think I ever had one real conversation with him and this was just part of the wreckage.

I know my dad always got up very early at 4:00 AM and left the house to open our family restaurant at 6:00 AM. There was always prep work to be started: baking to be done, coffee to be made, and cleaning from business the day before. He would work all day long through the breakfast rush, scrubbing pots and pans in-between the busy times. After getting walloped with the lunch crowd, and finally, dinner time would arrive until 6:00 or 7:00 PM, when he got caught up enough to come home and then it started all over again the next day. I remember you could get three vegetables and an entrée like roast turkey, beef with gravy, or meatloaf for practically nothing at his restaurant. He would come home after a long day, plop down on the floor, prop himself up with the sofa behind him, and sit right in front of the TV to unwind. His head would start to nod, and in no time, he would be fast asleep. Before long, mom would end up coaxing him to go upstairs to bed. I still can hear her voice to this day, "Pop, come on, get up, and go to bed; 4:00 AM comes early!"

I also remember how violently mad Pop would get when my middle sister would be on the telephone talking to her boyfriend while beautifying herself. You know, how teenage girls pluck their eyebrows and do all that girlie stuff? Pop would get mad at her for having the radio volume too loud, being on the phone, and so on. And don't let me forget how that one small bathroom light bulb would light up so brightly that the light would creep out from underneath the bathroom door and light the upstairs hallway like an airport runway. Dad always wanted it dark and dead quiet when he was trying to go to sleep.

I remember hiding my head under the covers, thinking I was going to get it next. I was scared to death of my dad, and this caused additional wreckage.

There were many things I was not thrilled about in my upbringing. But, I was thankful that this seasoned me in such a way to know that I never wanted to raise my children the same way I was raised. I never had a talk with my father about the opposite sex. I never had him read a story to me; we never talked baseball or any kind of sport for that matter. All this void or lack of interaction created some sort of wreckage in my life. After all, every child needs a parent that is present. I remember going to my friend's house on Sunday and watching the *Baltimore Colts* on their color TV—it was an incredible experience. Afterward, the first thing I did was run home and tell my dad—asking him, "Why don't we have a color TV?" His reaction was, "What do you want, blood from me? Here, take my arm!" But, he was always a great provider, there was no one ever going hungry in our household. We still lived in a beautiful warm home that we owned, he always drove a new automobile, and all us kids were clean and well dressed.

Another one of the few vivid memories of my father was, occasionally, he and my mother and I would take an early evening ride in the car—especially during daylight savings time. Dad loved his cars, and once in a while, he would allow someone else to handle the end of the dinner hour. This granted him the opportunity to go for a ride with mom and me— afterward, he would go back and close the restaurant. I remember mom and dad picking me up at the playground a block or so away from our house, and dad asking me if I wanted to go along for a ride. I had a brand new "JC Higgins red 20 bicycle" that Santa brought me the Christmas before. When he said "ride," I dropped that thing against the curb, and climbed into the back seat of his car. He immediately yelled, "Wait a minute! What are you doing, just leaving your bike lying against the curb!?" My reply was, "Santa brought me the bike, it's okay. It will be here when we get back." He retorted, "Who do you think Santa Clause is? I am Santa. Pick that bike up and put it in the trunk of the car!" Of course, I was devastated, I had no idea my dad was Santa. What did I know? I was five years old!

It bothered me that I missed out on the family picnics at Rocky Springs Park—the ones that my brothers and sisters always had the privilege to enjoy. Also, I never experienced the thrill of The Steel Pier in Atlantic City, New Jersey—it was just never a part of my life. I always said, "I was the surprise child, the last of six brothers and sisters!" Believe me, I would have hated to have been my mother when she had to tell my father she was pregnant and expecting another child. More wreckage; after all, I was the last of six, and there was six years difference between my sister—number three of the girls and myself. Everyone else in the family was "Wham bam, thank you, Ma'am!" Five children, one right after the other... then me at the tail end! Again, all this played some sort of role in surviving the wreckage.

On May 7th my father abandoned me and passed away. I was the one who discovered his cold, lifeless body lying in his bed. It was just before 7:00 AM on a Friday morning. I will never forget that day as long as I live. I remember checking his breathing, his heartbeat, but to no avail. Then trying to resuscitate him and breathe life into a relationship that was never there. He had passed away sometime in his sleep that early morning. I called the Doctor, the Coroner, and my brothers and sisters to tell them the news of Pop's death. I felt abandoned. All I wanted to do was catch the ball with him, talk, tell stories, and have fun with my dad! I didn't sign up for all this extra stuff. Pop was worn out, tired, old, stressed, shot, and now he had moved on and left behind six children, including the one he never knew and that would be me!

WHAT I MEANT TO SAY WAS...

Nevertheless, I managed to survive the wreckage and pretty much raised myself. I think, except for a little dysfunction here and there and some added drama on top, I turned out okay. It's amazing what you can become, and this is a true testament to what God can set out to do with a person.

"In you, LORD my God, I put my trust. I trust in you; do not let me be put to shame, nor let my enemies triumph over me" (Psalm 25:1-2).

I never wanted to be like my dad. But as much wreckage as I think he caused in our family, I could sort through the pieces and dissect the good that I could use! I always wanted to thank my dad for delivering my newspapers from one of the two paper routes that I had at the start of seventh grade, so I could play Junior High football. This only went on for a few nights, because it was just too much burden for me to place on him. Soon after, I quit the football team and resumed my morning and evening paperboy duties. The thought was great, and his intentions were so giving and wonderful, but he just wasn't that healthy at the time. Besides, it was just too hard on him physically—schlepping around with over 100 newspapers in a shoulder bag. This occurred in August or September, the year before he passed away.

I wanted to be a better dad than he was. I think each child has the desire to want to have it better than their parents had it and to provide better for their children. I wanted to be a better spiritual leader, a better parent, a better father, an example to my peers, fun, and a confidant to my children. At a young parenting age—much younger than my father was when I was conceived—I knew, I was going to be different than he was! Unlike my father, I was going to take my children to the lake, the pool, and the beach, as well as go on many vacations. I would teach them to play ball, ride a bicycle, and motorcycle with me. I would take them to work, to football games, teach them to water-ski, swim, and scuba dive. They would learn to be independent and an asset to society with life skills—ones that my father never had time to teach me.

I'm not sure how many of my skills I actually received from him. I think he did give me sticking power and the will to win. After all, he came from Eastern Europe at the ripe young age of 17 as a stow-away on a Greek Freighter Cargo Ship. Can you imagine? Having no food or a place to stay on board the ship, he had to hide all day long, and scavenge all night long. An immigrant, penny-less that couldn't speak a lick of English, and he made a life for himself in America! Without my dad, I wouldn't be here! When I think about it, could I have accomplished that? I don't think so!

I survived by forgiving him; I will honor him and love myself. I will not walk out on my children leaving them without the life skills that I was missing! Though he didn't have the kind of love that I have for my children, nevertheless he loved me the best way he could—his way! Now my Heavenly Father has all the love for me that I need and desire. I love and accept me unconditionally. Besides, I have friends and family that truly love me for who I am; nothing more and nothing less. Believe me, through thick and thin you'll learn who they are. God loves me, "Just as I am!" I'm determined to be a man of honesty and integrity in all situations.

I survived the wreckage by knowing that you are never alone. I will not be alone, I will not feel alone, and I will not feel abandoned by anyone in life ever again. I will be healthy and capable of being alone, and apart from my loved ones when necessary, for God has empowered me to do so. I made a clear choice and a decision to honor God, to honor my mate, and myself for the rest of my life. But that's not enough—I know I need to keep my face in the Word by reading my Bible, and my daily devotions. I also need to go to support groups if ever necessary again, attend church regularly, go to Bible studies, and much more! I know I need to have Faith—even my dad was a praying man. I remember him sitting on his bed every night praying to God.

Dad was not saying a word—he was just sitting there, puffing on his cigarette, flicking the ashes with his little finger, taking it all in. These were all the things that I meant to say to my dad. Today was the day that I got to talk to him about surviving the wreckage! As I spoke with my father at the cemetery, I looked at him and said, "Dad I wanted you to know I survived. I survived from what I believed was the wreckage of you not being around for me when I was at a formidable age." He replied, "I was never given a manual to operate a family correctly. I left my family, five brothers and sisters, my father and mother overseas, and I came to America with nothing but the clothing on my back. I built a legacy with six wonderful children here in America. Each one has made their own legacy, and each one has been an asset to society. I wasn't perfect, but just look how you and your brothers and sisters have all turned out." Dad continued, "My father never gave me the real-life lessons that I needed either, but I never complained, that was never allowed. I always wanted to spend time with you, but time got away from me with trying to provide a life for everyone. Business was tough, but I always knew you, of all my children, would make things happen in your life. I knew I never had to give you an instruction book for anything; you always could look at something, any situation, and figure out how to make it work correctly." "Wow!" I thought. "That made me feel so guilty; did I really have as much wreckage to survive as I thought?"

Time was getting on, and daylight was diminishing as I just sat back and decided to rest my eyes for a bit, on this beautiful day with my dad by my side. I was so thankful to have another chance to say what I meant and mean what I said.

How Can This Help You?

Have deep-rooted faith in all that you do! I know that Enoch, Noah, Abraham, Isaac, Jacob, Joseph, and even Moses all had to have the confidence to do what they did. By faith, the people passed through the Red Sea, and the walls of Jericho fell. Others escaped the mouth of lions, the belly of the whale, the fury of flames, the edge of the sword, and even Christ was crucified with faith! Still, others faced flogging, jeers, stoning, and Paul was imprisoned... why???? They all survived some sort of wreckage, but their faith kept them going. I know that I will get through the ups and downs in my life, all without teeth marks, without being whipped, without being persecuted or mistreated, or given a crown of thorns. God has something better planned for me, and He will not allow me to fail!

God expects perfection from each one of us.

"Whatever you do, work at it with all your heart, as working for the Lord, not for human masters, since you know that you will receive an inheritance from the Lord as a reward. It is the Lord Christ you are serving." (Colossians 3:23-24)

It's the Lord Jesus Christ we are serving! Treat everyone the same! It goes on to say a few verses later:

"Be wise in the way you act toward outsiders; make the most of every opportunity." (Colossians 4:5)

I always try to treat everyone the same—I don't care how much money they make or what color their skin is, or what they can or can't do for me. Make the most of every opportunity you are presented with. Let your conversation be always full of grace, seasoned with salt, so that you may know how to answer everyone.

Have compassion for all! But also a few chapters before it says:

"Therefore, as God's chosen people, holy and dearly loved, clothe yourselves with compassion, kindness, humility, gentleness, and patience." (Colossians 3:12)

The most incredible thing is that God chooses to love us despite our inevitable lapses, so this is why I say, "I survived the wreckage!"

Make family a priority! Set goals to spend quality time with your children, read to them, vacation with them, play sports together. Tell them you love them often; but most of all, share the Gospel and go to church with them.

Don't duplicate bad decisions learned from your parents! Unfortunately, we as parents don't always make the best decisions possible. Get plugged into a group of accountable men either at church or in a Bible study group that has experience in being faithful to God's word! And women, this is true for you, as well. Children grow up to be like their parents, make sure you are a good parent!

Chapter 5

CALL THE AMBULANCE, THIS CHILD IS ABOUT TO DIE!

I am being loaded into a Cadillac ambulance; one that looks just like the one right out of the movie *Ghostbusters*. I had missed several weeks of first grade going from doctor to doctor, each doctor trying to diagnose what on earth was ailing me? I have no color, no appetite, I can't keep food down, I have a high fever, and I am losing weight by the day!

After two weeks of absence from the classroom, it took the fourth-grade school nurse and Principal to come to the house and check on me during a routine visit to discover that my appendix had burst. And it was now spilling infectious materials into the abdominal cavity of my skinny body! My lifeless body was jaundiced and sapped of all strength. The school nurse barked orders to my mother, "Call an ambulance immediately, this child has a burst appendix!"

I can feel the ambulance speeding across the Fourth Street railroad tracks. It's not my first trip across those tracks speeding to the hospital. Between practically biting my tongue off a couple of years earlier after using my bed as a trampoline, nearly choking to death after swallowing a whole piece of hard candy, and several broken arms, I think I was on a first name basis with the administration staff, nurses, and doctors of the local hospital.

The head surgeon met the ambulance at the emergency room doors where I was quickly whisked off to the operating room. I don't think anyone can be entirely sure what that three-and-a-half-inch long tube of tissue that extends from the large intestine does or what the function of the appendix is. One thing, I do know: I am living proof you can live without it, without any apparent consequence!

I am five years old, and I remember waking up inside an oxygen tent. It's a pretty strange feeling looking out through that plastic box that surrounds you. Now I know how "Bubble Boy" felt in *Seinfeld*. Tubes connected to me everywhere and as I was told it was give-and-take for a few days. The way I understand it, I'm pretty lucky to be here and be alive. I didn't retain my spot in the oxygen tent for long, the next day Doc sent me back to the operating room to open up the other side of my tummy because I had all this infectious material spilling into my abdominal cavity that he initially thought would be cleared up with some strong antibiotics.

I was in the hospital for quite some time and missed over 50 days of school, but they can't hold me down, I know that for sure. I know, I must have nine lives after this episode, four broken arms, fractured fingers, ankles, and a multitude of other stitches, cuts, bruises, and car and train wrecks weren't about to stop me.

As I grew a little older, I had many influential people in my life—like my Junior High shop teacher. He was not only the industrial arts and shop teacher but also the softball coach at the local playground. I was always one of his favorites. He taught me how to be a great first baseman and an even better hitter. Considering all the many times I tried out for Little League there was never a coach that thought I had enough talent to play hardball for any of their teams. But I did turn out to be one of the best softball players from all the different playground softball teams and a great team captain!

Then there were others like my science teacher, who punched me in the mouth in seventh grade because I was such a smart aleck. And who could forget my health teacher and basketball coach? He was another one of those teachers that squeezed every ounce of effort out of me just like my eighth and ninth grade varsity basketball coach.

I'll never forget we were playing at home at the high school and I played nearly the entire game; in fact, I think it was my best game ever. But he pulled me out late in the fourth quarter to give some of the other players playing time. I never thought I was going back in the game, so I proceeded to take off my sneakers, and about that time the guy that replaced me was getting eaten alive under the back-boards. Thus, the coach called me to go back in the game. All of a sudden, he looked down at my feet and noticed my sneakers were off. Wow, if looks could kill, I would have been dead instantly!

But there wasn't a teacher like our music teacher; she was this big-voiced gal who was the music instructor in Junior High. Her brother was the choir director at the church I attended, and of course, I sang with her three sons. Whenever she would introduce me, she would always say, "And this is our own professional singer—that's right class—Billy is a paid professional singer!" I had lots of opportunities for smiles in those days, these individuals that positively influenced my life were beyond special!

WHAT I MEANT TO SAY WAS...

I knew from a very young age that I was special. I don't see how children can detect that, but I knew I was unique from early on. I wasn't the best athlete, the smartest kid, and I didn't come from money, but I was always loved by my mother, brothers, and sisters and I made friends quickly. I was bound for something great. I guess I look at how Jesus chose His disciples; Christ chose the most unlikely characters: like Peter, the fisherman, and look at Matthew, the tax-collector, who would literally extort travelers from their money. I guess that is why He chose me, not because I intend to extort people, but in the eyes of the public I would have headed the list: "The most likely to not succeed!" Oh, boy, I remember being called a dreamer in high school and that daydreaming would never get me anywhere. But somehow, I dreamed big, and I turned those dreams into reality.

But along the way I had some incredibly influential people in my life; and while I really was a little wise guy, I had these various people that saw beyond my smart remarks and strange sense of humor. I can think about virtually every grade school teacher and how each one played a special part in me growing up and how each one was special and loving to me including the Principal that discovered my burst appendix.

My first-grade teacher who spanked my hands with the ruler and would make me hold dictionaries with my arms spread out. Yes, that was then, in first grade. I don't think the teachers today would try that? My second grade teach always enjoyed my company so much that I would visit her on my bike ride home from the community pool during summer break. My third grade teacher was a real favorite; I would steal the neighbor's flowers that were planted outside her fence row, never realizing at the time that they belonged to the neighbor until my mother asked me one day where I was getting the flowers for my teacher? Whoops!

There were many of these individuals that had a hand in molding my personality.

These inspiring verses come to mind:

"Indeed, the very hairs of your head are all numbered. Don't be afraid; you are worth more than many sparrows." (Luke 12:7)

"Before I formed you in the womb I knew you, before you were born I set you apart; I appointed you as a prophet to the nations." (Jeremiah 1:5)

And lastly, He chose me; I didn't choose Him!

"For he chose us in him before the creation of the world to be holy and blameless in his sight. In love he predestined us for adoption to sonship through Jesus Christ, in accordance with his pleasure and will." (Ephesians 1:4-5)

Wow, after that doctor saved my life, I developed a debt of gratitude towards him. I would run into him occasionally at the grocery store, the golf course, or a fundraising event. I always thanked him for his life-saving operation. I grew up in a small town, and there weren't that many patients to remember, but I know he never forgot my name, and Doc always addressed me by my name.

How Can This Help You?

I think as I grew older and more productive in my life, these individuals kept me somewhat grounded. It always made me realize that no matter how insignificant something may seem to you, it may be quite significant to someone else. You never know how you're going to touch someone's life, touch it well, you never know who's watching or paying attention!

Chapter 6

THE DROPOUT—
A FORM OF SELF-DELUSION

I find myself in the office of the Vice Principal of our high school. I was waiting for the outcome of my fist fight in the hall with my onetime friend from cub scouts, boy scouts. A friendship that went as far back as fifth grade. I fidgeted in my seat as memories from earlier in the day came flooding back to me.

It was the early part of April, and I was in the 11th grade. It was just after lunch, and I was on my way to my first afternoon class. There was always lots of commotion in the halls while passing from one class to the next. But this day was different; I was nearing my end with school, and just one mishap from being expelled permanently. Between in-school suspensions, 52 days absent, and probably equally as many days tardy, I was skating on mighty thin ice with the school administration and with the next wrong move, and I would be out on my ear!

While on my way to class I happened to be clowning around with a friend—we were slap boxing, or as some would call it, shadow boxing. I happened to get a little too close to "Biggy." Biggy was a 6' 2" monster of a guy with about as much coordination as an opossum on roller skates. But as I threw a right cross, Biggy backed up into my longtime friend and pinched his arm in his locker, and that's when it all started!

For some reason, this "friend" had been carrying a tremendous amount of anger towards me, and I'm not sure why. As youngsters we were quite friendly, and good kids. As I said, we were in cub scouts together; we played baseball and did all kinds of kid things together with never an unkind word towards each other. As his arm got pinched in his locker, he came unglued and proceeded to get in my face telling me he was tired of my crap! "Tired of my crap? What did I ever do to you?", I innocently asked. He replied, "I'm tired of you and your thinking how tough you are. Get ready for a real ass-kicking, because I've had it with you!" Wow... I was stunned, I knew deep down inside if I got into any kind of trouble, I was going to be outside looking in! He said, "So what's it going to be, here and now? Or, am I going to kick your butt after school?"

I had a million thoughts rambling through my mind at that moment. "I don't want to be a dropout. I don't need any more trouble than I've already caused myself this year. I don't want to give my mother anything to be ashamed of..." and a whole lot more. I placed my hands on his chest, and I said, "I don't need any more trouble. I really don't want to fight with you. I thought we were friends?" After I placed my hands on his chest, he pushed me and kept pushing me until I was up against the locker on the other side of the hallway. That's when I had enough! Without saying a word, I hit him with a right jab to his left cheek, followed by an immediate left to his lower chin.

Finally, ending with a strong right cross to his nose. With all the force of my body, I pushed my arm and fist deep into his face.

I took half a step, backing away. My opponent immediately grabbed his face with both hands holding his nose as blood gushed out between his fingers and ran down his forearms, arms, and into his sleeves. Blood was dripping everywhere. He looked like a stuffed pig that was just poked; blood was squishing out everywhere, from his nose, his mouth, and everywhere in between! Oh, how I didn't need this—boy was I in trouble. Why couldn't I have had more composure? Why did I have to hit him? I knew I could take him, why did I hit him? He started to run to the boy's lavatory about 50 feet away with a trail of blood to follow. All I wanted was to get out of there. My fifth-period class was starting in a minute or two, so I hustled to my class down the hall and immediately went in and quietly took my seat. There was a lot of static in the room: "Man, did you see how he hit him?" "Bam, Boom, Pow, and he was down and out for the count!" I wasn't thinking about all the admiration for my fighting skills. All I kept thinking about was, "How serious did I hurt my onetime friend?" And, "Boy, I'm going to be in trouble now!"

About 25 minutes had gone by in class when there was a knock at the classroom door with a message for our teacher. He read it and looked up me and said, "Young man, you're wanted in the Principal's office, now!"

I grabbed my books and headed out of the classroom; feeling so lonely, feeling like my life was over, feeling quite overwhelmed that my school days might soon be finished. Even though I had no interest in school, I never wanted to be that self-delusional dropout, thinking that I could go anywhere from here without even as much as a high school diploma.

I opened the door to the administration office of the Principal and the Vice-Principal and was immediately welcomed by their secretary. The first words out of her mouth were, "I think you're really in trouble this time!" I liked her, I think she understood me and was always kind towards me, but she has witnessed way too many of my trips to the office this year.

She opened the door to the Vice Principal's office and asked him, "Your guest is here, are you ready to see him?" "Yes, send him in; and ask the principal to join us!", came the reply from the office. When I overheard the tone of his command, I knew I had about as much chance as a waxed cat in hell of getting out of there alive!

She turned around as she gripped the doorway, smiled, and told me, "They are ready to see you." I walked in, tail tucked between my legs, knowing I was going to suffer the consequences of my actions. Before I could even sit down, the principal entered the adjoining office. Both these guys were tough disciplinarians. One had a tough-ass attitude and swaggered through the halls with this big chip on his shoulder. The other was the Principal—the new sheriff in town. He was large and in charge! He was a little more reserved. He was one of those—let me make sure I have all the facts—kind of guys. I felt like I had less than a slight chance in that room with these two guys. I felt like it was going to be a good cop-bad cop scenario, and I was about to get my head slammed into the desk.

I sat down facing the two of them from the weak side of the desk; head down in shame, arms folded across my chest, ready to hear the results of my scuffle. The Vice Principal spoke directly to me with the temperament of a seasoned drill sergeant. The Principal sat back, arms folded, holding his chin up with right-hand forefinger pointing straight up his cheek to his temple just taking it all in.

His first words were, "Did you know your classmate is on his way to the hospital with a broken nose and possible concussion? Do you realize that we have no place for this kind of behavior in this school of learning?!" He never even asked me my side of the story or my opinion of what happened in the hallway. He looked at the Principal, and then said, "I think this young man is finished for this school year." Looking at me, he then said "If you want, you could pay tuition and finish this year at one of the other high schools in town; but, considering your 52 days absent and your failing grades, they'll never take you at this point in the year. Do you agree, sir?" "Oh, yes, I agree!" I managed to stammer. "You could always come back next year, but we don't want you back here!" he loudly concluded. None of these suggestions for my future seemed like they were anything that I wanted to hear at this point. The Vice Principal continued, "Think about your actions, and on Monday we would like to meet with you and your mother to talk about your situation and your future from this point forward."

I have to tell you, I was relieved! I hated school. I loved the girls, loved cars, and now, this was my chance to get out of there and make something of myself. I never realized at that particular moment that education was the foundation I needed to make something of myself. I spent the entire weekend working on my mother, selling her on the idea that it was okay for me to drop out. I could find a job, maybe even join the Navy, sail the seven seas, and finish my education there! After all, I was just barely 17 years old and knew all of life's answers at this point. I remember that weekend as mom, and I talked about it, while my oldest brother voiced his opinion. Of course, he was 13 years my elder, a college graduate with a fabulous career with the electric company. His exact words were "You're nothing but a punk, and you're never going to amount to anything!" Words like this you never forget, they cut to the quick, and stick with you like a warm bowl of oatmeal on a cold morning!

Monday afternoon my mother and I drove to school to meet with the high school Principals. When we arrived, their secretary expressed to my mother that, "Billy is bright but bored with formal education, and he will find himself one day soon and make something great of himself!" A gigantic smile came upon my face, and my thought was, "Why don't other people see me like this?" She informed the dynamic duo of principals that we were there, and they immediately invited us in to sit down. The introductions were, well, let me say phony on their part—at least, on the VP's part. All he wanted was a troublemaker like me out of his hair, and he didn't care if I was one more high school dropout statistic.

SELF-DECEPTION AND DELUSIONAL THINKING— WHAT I MEANT TO SAY WAS...

If you want to experience hard knocks, then drop out of school. Go ahead it's easy! It seems I was now taking a ride on the bus to low life High! I loved my mother more than anything in the world, but I did a selling job on her. What I meant to say to her at the time was, "Mom you should have been tougher on me and grabbed me by the nap of the collar and marched my delinquent butt back to school. I wish you would have said to the dynamic duo principals, 'this child will finish school this year, and between the three of us, we must watch this child graduate, and not become a dropout statistic! I will be accountable, you will be accountable, and most of all, he will be accountable and finish this year and next year, and with passing grades. No more days of absence. Is that clearly understood?!'"

Well, I did drop out, and it was quickly proven that I didn't know it all. In fact, I didn't know diddly! I had eight jobs from April until the end of that first year but wrongly thought, "I must be doing something right to be able to jump from job to job without missing a beat."

This form of self-delusion allowed me to be deceived into believing I knew it all! This attitude has caused more individuals a tremendous amount of problems. Self-deception or delusional thinking is a process of denying or rationalizing away the relevance, significance, or importance of opposing evidence, and the logical side of the argument! Self-deception involves convincing oneself of truth or lack of truth so that one does not reveal any self-knowledge of the deception. This can apply to drugs, women, pornography, and a hundred other things that we choose to ignore the signs that are about to be our demise!

I ran into the Vice Principal many years later. He was retired and playing golf in a local golf tournament, benefiting the education system from his former high school and the local college. I was one of the sponsors of the competition. By this time in my career, I had been in 100s of radio and TV commercials; I also had been heavily involved in community events and boards, as well as, my downtown revitalization project, and I had become a pretty visible guy in the community. I remember him coming up to me, shaking my hand, and saying, "You really have made something great of yourself!" My immediate thought was, "Yeah, no thanks to you, buddy!" But having long since laid the woundedness of my past at the cross, I thanked him and said that was very kind of him and wished him well in the golf tournament. After the golf tournament he approached me and said he wished he would have worked harder at getting to the issues with me instead of allowing me drop out of school!

HOW CAN THIS HELP YOU?

Avoid self-delusion and self-deception at all costs. Don't allow that nasty little voice in your head telling you it's okay to go down the wrong road! Let me share a good story with you that a lifelong friend shared with me when I was going through really tough times. Have you ever heard the story of "The Devil's Yard Sale?"

There was a huge community yard sale, and Satan had his stand all set up. He had a table full of tools, some tools more worn than others, but a wide variety of weapons. There was the tool of Discouragement, Deception, and Self-Delusion. Also, the tool of Abortion, the tool of Hardship, Depression, Divorce, and many others spread out on his table of wares. A man walked up and priced some of the old tools, and finally came across one particular tool of interest. It was worn so hard, with a battered handle and a well-worn head; you could tell it had a lot of use, a lot more than most others on the pile. He asked Satan, "What was this tool?" Satan replied, "This is the tool of Self-Delusion." The man asked, "What is the price of this particular tool?" Satan proceeded to tell him: "Oh, this is the most expensive tool I sell!" The man replied... "Why is that? It's worn, shot, and it looks like it has very little use left in it?" Then Satan replied, "No... you see the tool of Self-Delusion or Self-Deception will work when all others fail, that's why it's worn so hard! If I can't get them with all the other tools, 'Discouragement, Deception, and Self-Delusion' will always work."

Today, if you feel like Satan is using his tool of Discouragement, Deception, or Self-Delusion on you or someone you know, listen to what Nathan Lustig has to say about this:

"We are all humans; we all make mistakes and have strengths and weaknesses. Everyone has areas where they need to improve. But they are hard to identify, and it is even harder to make the changes necessary to improve. It's hard because of self-deception. It's part of our automatic human defense mechanism. It is there precisely to prevent us from getting hurt. But to grow and have success, humans must be able to identify the points in their lives when they're lying to themselves. If not, you'll keep bouncing around in life until the nonsense finally hits the fan and you're forced to face facts."

He goes on to say:

"Self-Deception is the fountain of failure, unhappiness, and missed opportunities. Identifying when you have been deceiving yourself and then why you have been doing it are the keys to improving the situation. It's true in all facets of life, from work to friends to family to learning a new skill."

Be sure to put on the full armor of God!

"Finally, be strong in the Lord and in his mighty power. Put on the full armor of God, so that you can take your stand against the devil's schemes. For our struggle is not against flesh and blood, but against the rulers, against the authorities, against the powers of this dark world and against the spiritual forces of evil in the heavenly realms. Therefore, put on the full armor of God, so that when the day of evil comes, you may be able to stand your ground, and after you have done everything, to stand. Stand firm then, with the

belt of truth buckled around your waist, with the breastplate of righteousness in place, and with your feet fitted with the readiness that comes from the gospel of peace. In addition to all this, take up the shield of faith, with which you can extinguish all the flaming arrows of the evil one. Take the helmet of salvation and the sword of the Spirit, which is the word of God." (Ephesians 6:10–18)

Chapter 7

In-A-Gadda-Da-Vida

Beep, Beep, Beep, Beep, Beep, Beep, Beep! I reach from my bed to turn off my alarm. It's dark in the room and nice and warm underneath my covers. I'm trying to get awake; I know I have to get going and go to work. I slowly become more conscious of my surroundings. Oh, my word! I look at the clock, it is 6:40 AM. I now hear my buddy Jake blowing his car horn outside my house, trying to signal me to ride to work with him!

Late November weather produces some chilly mornings, too cold to ride a motorcycle to work. My one co-worker had become a great friend, offering to take me to and from work on chilly or rainy days. Even though it sometimes would make him tardy due to my lack of work ethic and being able to get up on a timely basis, he still came and picked me up for work.

It turned out he had been blowing his car horn for 10 minutes outside my door, so we could drive to work and not be late! I sprang from the bed, grabbed my jeans, work boots, shirt, jacket, and a few other necessary things, and out the door I went.

I jumped the fence in the backyard catapulting my way to the street, grabbed the door handle as quickly as possible. I pulled the door open and jumped into the warm car as soon as I could, so I wouldn't make him any later than what we already were that morning. My buddy loved his music, especially rock n' roll—as most kids do. The eight-track stereo was blaring, the car vibrating from the loud speakers. Iron Butterfly was playing on the eight-track that morning.

Fortunately, we only lived a couple of miles from work, so it would just take a few minutes to get there. Hopefully, we would make it for the 7:00 AM punch-in time at the machine shop we worked at. We pulled out of the street that I lived on and took a left turn on to Fourth Street. About a block south we were welcomed by the downed railroad crossing gate, blinking lights, and the ding, ding, ding, ding of the crossing gate bell—all signs of, "Beware, Do Not Cross the Gates, Danger!"

In-A-Gadda-Da-Vida was now the next song on the play-set, and it was the perfect song for what was about to unfold!

If you are familiar with the lyrics of this famous rock-n-roll song, this song was written by Doug Ingle—Iron Butterfly's vocalist and keyboard player. His father was a church organist.

The title was supposed to be, "In the Garden of Eden." Someone had written on a demo copy—possibly while drunk or high—the words, "In-A-Gadda-Da-Vida." A record company executive saw it and decided to use it as the album's title song!

The crossing gates were down, the lights blinking on and off... Ding, ding, dinging bells continued to ring loud and clear in the foggy morning. As you might know sound travels better and faster in fog. Foggy conditions also have an ambient dampening effect on the sound waves, making it eerie and quieter than it really is. Time was getting on; it was nearly 6:50 AM—10 minutes until the time we clock in! If we were going to be on time for work, the train had to come quickly and pass by, or we had to run the gates before the train arrived at the Fourth Street crossing. The Fourth Street crossing is one of the broadest railroad crossings in town; it has six or seven sets of railroad tracks crossing the street. We rolled down the windows, turned down the stereo, and listened quietly. The wind just happened to be blowing the sound of the train to the east, but the train was coming from the east heading westbound! We couldn't see anything, we couldn't hear anything. The darkness and the thick November morning fog blocked everything from our view!

"Do you hear something?" I whispered. "I don't hear anything." My buddy responded. He dropped the car into reverse, backed up, popped it back into drive, and gunned the gas to move around the downed-blinking crossing gates. He turned the stereo back up, "In a gadda da vida, baby." The music blaring as we crossed the first set of tracks, then the second set of tracks, when and all of a sudden, BAM! There was a massive, crushing blow when the train slammed into the left side of the car! The sound of screeching brakes and wheels from the powerful train engine, breaking glass splashing everywhere, the sound of crushing metal, and smashing car parts screeched and erupted in our ears.

It was like we were in slow motion, In... a... gadda... da... vida... baby, played loudly, as the car was picked up and hurled into the fog-filled black air landing three sets of railroad tracks over and pushed all the way down to Fifth Street. As the car came to a heaping rest, I knew I was okay. The train hit the driver's side, just behind the front door, catching the rear quarter panel of the Oldsmobile with a hard blow. My friend didn't know if he was poorly hurt or not; he was stunned. The car ste-reo still playing, "Don't you know that I'm lovin' you." I got out of the car. There were car parts strewn everywhere: the rear axle, wheels, and driveshaft scattered across the tracks. The gas tank lay motionless, just waiting for a spark to ignite it with a huge explosion. The entire back end of the car was lying lifeless almost a city block away. I immediately ran to the driver's door to help him escape from the wreckage, in his much-shaken state of con-fusion. Seconds later, the conductor and engineer are running toward us, yelling, "Is everyone okay?!" People quickly gathered around us from the other side of the street amazed that we were both alive. Moments later fire trucks arrived on the scene as well as the emergency crew. They quickly loaded us both into the ambulance to take us to the nearby hospital for observation. The doctors gave both of us sedatives, and we promptly passed out from all the excitement.

QUESTION YOURSELF—
WHAT I MEANT TO SAY WAS...

I should have never put a friend in a position that could have compromised his life. My selfishness of not going to bed earlier, so I could get a decent night of sleep, placed him and myself in a bad situation. I took advantage of his generosity, even to the point that he possibly could have been fired for being late, let alone almost losing his life because of me! And then to think about all the costs he had to absorb, from wrecking his automo-bile to rising insurance costs from the total loss—all out of my selfishness to not get out of bed on time.

Sometimes it's just not your time to meet your Maker. Sometimes God is not going to allow something severe to come between His ultimate plans for you—even to the point of giving mercy and grace when you do something foolish. But let me add,

I don't recommend testing God's patience or will. Let's face it; His plan is never our plan!

"For I know the plans I have for you,' declares the LORD, 'plans to prosper you and not to harm you, plans to give you hope and a future.'" (Jeremiah 29:11)

When something tragic could have altered the balance of your life, maybe it's time to question yourself and look to God and see what He has in store for you.

HOW CAN THIS HELP YOU?

That dark, cold morning, I never set out to have a friend's life almost taken and have his car destroyed beyond recognition. We never intend for bad things to happen, but poor choices practically always produce poor results. With selfish actions and putting our needs before the needs of others, there is still a price to pay—not sometime, but always! It took a long time for me to realize everything in this world is not about me!

Today let's try on a dose of humility for a change: allow people who deal with you through business, friendship, relationships, or whatever to see Christ through you. Give them the Wows! Make them say as they walk away from doing business with you... "Wow!" Make them sense that there is something different about this person and I want what he or she has.

Chapter 8

My Boy,
You Talk too Much

I was taking a little power nap at a table of the machine shop I worked at. During the lunch break, I could usually dose in and out for five or 10 minutes before we went back to work. You know how late nights can be? One right after another, burning the candle at both ends as they say, and I was pretty good at getting the most out of a 24-hour day.

I had been jumping from job to job since I dropped out of high school the previous year. I held seven or eight different positions during this eight-month period of my life. I did about everything you could think of, including working for a moving company, loading furniture, and carrying heavy furniture up and down several flights of steps. Oh, that was good, I was about 150 pounds soaking wet, and I was really comfortable with a 150-pound dresser on my back going up three flights of rickety old steps! I moved around the county. For one job, I loaded a blast furnace with scrap metal. Again, here I am, a light-weight guy, loading and moving a 600-pound wheel-barrow full of scrap metal and dumping it into a 2500-degree molten lava pit. The jobs I had held down as a young kid were not what I would call the best jobs in the marketplace, or for that fact, any kind of a situation that one day would support a family.

The machine shop was kind enough to hire me, especially, since I had several other jobs doing similar work. The owner of the machine shop was a beaten-down man; hard looking, and twice as hard working. He appeared as though he had been at it for 100 years. He prowled around his dimly lit machine company, filled with barely operating lathes, drill presses, and so on. His eyes were always looking over his spark etched safety-glasses, which were loaded with smudges and filthy dirty. I'm not sure how he could even read a micrometer through those things! His feet dragged his tired old body over the oil soaked, black, shop floors checking on the various jobs, moving about from employee to employee.

When he wasn't in the shop, you would find him in the main office. His wife worked side-by-side with him. She handled employee records, billing, payroll, and anything else associated with bookkeeping.

I was hired by the old man, and believe me, I was thrilled to have a job. He promised me a machinist's apprenticeship, which turned out to be a total crock of crap. I was a high school drop-out, and he said, "My boy, you need your high school diploma for your machinist's license!" Another crock of crap, as it turns out. So, with his advice, I went to the city high school office and took the G.E.D. test. I actually took the test and received my diploma before my class graduated, and I received the highest score at the time ever posted in the school district, at least, that's what the teacher told me that was administering the test.

I did anything imaginable at that machine shop, from driving the company truck to counties far and wide delivering goods that we would manufacture for clients. I operated about every machine in the building, including drill-presses, lathes, milling machines, and so on. But the worst job I have ever had in my life was operating the abrasive cutoff saw. Environmentally speaking, the shop should have been closed down for the impurities that are spewed into the air, and frankly, it's a wonder that I don't have mesothelioma—asbestos poisoning—from operating that machine. What a health hazard! Picture someone wearing a black vinyl coated, hooded sweatshirt to keep the sparks from going down their shirt, a pair of welder's goggles to protect the eyes, and a full-face respirator to prevent breathing excessive asbestos dust. I probably looked like Ralph McQuarrie's first creation of "Darth Vader" created for George Lucas in *Star Wars*. The worst thing was the awful smoke, dust, and the smell that terrible machine put off when you operated it. But whatever I was asked to do, I always did it without complaining.

One day the old man called me into his office a month or two after going to work for him. He said to me, "My Boy, we are going to give you a 10 cent an hour raise next week, you're doing a nice job." Another crock of crap. They were forced to give me a raise when the minimum wage jumped. Wow, that made my hourly wage $2.10 an hour, exactly what the United States Government minimum wage was increased to!

A few months had passed, and I thought, I fit in pretty well at the machine shop. We had our occasional Friday afternoon cake celebrations, and they would honor someone for years of service or sing happy birthday to someone. But after one of the typical end-of-day celebrations, I got the dreaded call into the front office. I knew there was no way of getting another 10 cent an hour raise so soon—it had to be bad news. He said to me, "My boy, I got to let you go... you talk too much!" I was devastated. I had already worked at three or four different machine shops in the last year, now I didn't know what I was going to do. His comment to me was, "Did you ever think about going into sales? You have a great gift of gab." Now, that I know something about selling, guys that talk too much usually talk themselves' right out of the sale!

Luckily, a few months before my unplanned departure from the machine shop, I had started working part-time at one of the local service stations, so at least I had a part-time job to fall back on. It's funny how things work out. We never know what's around the corner, or what God has in store for us. Sometimes we get so worked up in our situation that we never look around and say, "Thanks, God! I know You always know what's best for me. If You're going to take me away from operating a dirty, abrasive, cutoff saw, and plop me into sales, I'm fine with that!" We don't always know what the outcome will be in life. I didn't realize that my gas station job would catapult me into sales somehow. When I think about it, it was sales... selling tires, batteries, oil changes, and more.

Psalm 91 says...

"If you say, 'The LORD is my refuge,' and you make the Most High your dwelling, no harm will overtake you, no disaster will come near your tent. For he will command his angels concerning you to guard you in all your ways; they will lift you up in their hands so that you will not strike your foot against a stone. You will tread on the lion and

the cobra; you will trample the great lion and the serpent."
(Psalm 91: 9-13)

OPPORTUNITY DISGUISED AS DISASTER— WHAT I MEANT TO SAY WAS...

What I really wanted to tell the old man at the machine shop was, "You know, sir, the working conditions suck here at your machine shop! And while I'm at it, the lighting is poor too. And Frankly, I don't know how you manage to keep any employees at all. You pay terrible, and the working environment is so poor, it's a wonder half your employees are still here! So, thanks for making me realize that I have better opportunities out there, and maybe, just maybe, I will go buy a book and start to learn what I can about selling!"

As it turned out, he was really the last guy that I worked for in my life. From then on, I was self-employed or worked as a commissioned sales person, having no one but myself to determine how much money I was going to make or how far up the leadership ladder I was going to go! Sometimes an opportunity can be disguised as a disaster, and it is our job to decipher the difference.

HOW CAN THIS HELP YOU?

Sometimes, we don't know what we need, want, or where God intends us to be. Sometimes, God has to pave the way for us, and believe me when you are out of God's will, the road can be plenty bumpy! I guess, if we were doing the planning, we would be riding in a fancy limousine and having God, his angels, or disciples showing us that this or that is about to happen but don't worry! And then he says "Do you see that corner down there? If you do this in your life, you are going to have some rough riding ahead!" Don't you wish it was that simple? I think it really is that simple if we obey and follow God's word. My best advice at this point would be this verse from I Corinthians:

> *"So whether you eat or drink or whatever you do, do it all for the glory of God."* (1 Corinthians 10:31)

Chapter 9

When the Door of Opportunity Knocks

I'm sitting in front of the executive desk facing Morgan J. Maxwell Sr. and to his right, his son M.J. Maxwell Jr., who I've come to know as MJ, or Morg, and sometimes Junior. At that time, I had no idea that the gas station I worked at part-time would oust the current dealer-operator manager because of a little stealing here and there! I just happened to be in line for my first business venture at age 18; at least, Junior thought I was 18 years old!

Morgan loved the way I treated and catered to my customers on the service island. The island was the gas pump area where customers would pull up to and have their gas pumped in those days. This was long before self-service gas stations came into being. I would come to know the service area as Paradise. Why Paradise? Because it was so comfortable there. I was great at making things happen on the island: getting service appointments, selling tires, sales of just about anything like oil changes, wiper blades, state inspections, and so on. I loved talking with the customers as I cleaned their windshields, pumped their gas, as I would molly-coddle them with excellent service.

Morgan Jr. and Morgan Sr. thought I would make a great dealer-operator at one of their service stations; after all, I was familiar with the operation having worked there for several months. Morgan said he would teach me a few of the financial things he thought, I would be good at it, and good at it I was.

I would buy the necessary tools. I needed to have a licensed state inspection station and pass the state inspection test. Soon we were doing state inspections and all kinds of mechanical work from engine-rebuilds, brakes, and exhaust systems. You name it, and we did it! Now, understand, I had no formal training as an auto mechanic; in fact, I tried getting a job at the local Chevrolet dealership in town, and the service manager said, "Do you have any auto mechanic experience?" "No!" I replied. "Did you have any formal auto shop education?" To both of the questions, I had to answer a big fat, "NO!" But, I was determined to make something of myself. I was tired of jumping from job to job, and I loved cars. The funny thing is that very same service manager just 10 years later would end up working for me.

Business was booming, we didn't sell as much gas as some of our competitors, but our service work was multiplying. I started doing work for the local newspaper, and a couple of radio stations. All of the work I did for them, I put on an account. I traded and escrowed their expenditures into an advertising account. When the time came for a big event or an anniversary sale, I had all the advertising dollars stockpiled! My line of thinking was, "What will make new customers want to visit my service station?" I came up with the idea of having a tire sale—not just a tire sale—but the tire sale of tire sales in my area.

I didn't have the money to go out and buy a lot of inventory for this event, but I knew if it was going to be successful, we had to make it look like we had a massive amount of product. I went to four or five of the big tire distributors that I knew in our area, and I consigned tires from them. I hauled truckloads of tires and consigned them at great prices, so I could have some great price leaders. I had an old Chevy pickup truck at the time, and for weeks on end, I would travel to different distributors and pick up loads of tires. My days were filled with selling gas and repairing cars, then picking up tires at night! Once I had so many tires piled and roped into the back of my pickup truck, they stood four feet above the roof. When I did my display at the gas station, we had 100s of tires stacked everywhere, huge banners, sale flyers for the windows, and flyers printed out for anyone that came in for gasoline. Also, we had flyers made for the windshields of all the cars from the surrounding shopping centers. While I was working the island, I made sure to pitch the sale too!

The clothing store next to my gas station always had aggressive print ads. I was privileged to see their newspaper ads all the time. They were some pretty hard-hitting ads compared to the typical clothing store. So, I mimicked their print ad with a massive sheet of white paper that I taped together to make the size of a full-page newspaper ad. I copied their ad content using what I wanted, taking photos of piles of tires, and using those as well with some incredible loss-leaders! Also, I put together some hard-hitting radio commercials and a couple of the radio stations as well to do live broadcasts to promote the event on the spot! This would be my first experience at speaking on the radio or doing radio commercials at 18 years old.

One of my price leaders would be, "Four tires, mounted, balanced, and Installed for $59! That's pretty cheap, isn't it?" Of course, it was a 560 x 15 size tire that fit a Volkswagen, but I was about to show our area how to up-sell tires! Now understand, this was four tires that cost me at the time $15.00 each. In essence, I had $60 invested in four tires, my labor to pick them up, mount the tires, balance them, and get rid of the old tires. I'll bet you're thinking, no wonder you sold tires at that price! But not everyone drove a Volkswagen or a small car that fit such a small tire. I sold 100s of other tires that weekend, service work, and state inspections booked for weeks on end. When the dust settled, I made over $3,000 profit in one four-day weekend!

SHAKE IT OFF AND STEP UP— WHAT I MEANT TO SAY WAS...

For the first time in my life, it allowed me to be in charge of me and figure out how to get out of the hole and unleash my creative genius on my own. I guess I've been doing that my entire life. This reminds me of the old fable of the farmer's donkey that falls into the well. It is worth telling the story.

One day, a farmer's donkey fell down into a well. The animal cried piteously for hours as the farmer tried to figure out a way to get him out. Finally, he decided it was probably impossible, and the animal was old, and the well was dry anyway. It just wasn't worth it to try and retrieve the donkey. So, the farmer asked his neighbors to come over and help him cover up the well. They all grabbed shovels and began to shovel dirt into the well.

At first, when the donkey realized what was happening, he cried horribly. Then, to everyone's amazement, he quieted down and let out some happy brays. A few shovel loads later, the farmer looked down the well to see what was happening and was astonished at what he saw. With every shovel of dirt that hit his back, the donkey was shaking it off and taking a step up.

As the farmer's neighbors continued to shovel dirt on top of the animal, he continued to shake it off and take a step up. Pretty soon, to everyone's amazement, the donkey stepped up over the edge of the well and trotted off!

Moral: Life is going to shovel dirt on you. The trick to getting out of the well is to shake it off and take a step up. Every adversity can be turned into a stepping stone. The way to get out of the deepest well is by never giving up, but by shaking yourself off, and taking a step up.

As I would say "Life is 10% of what happens to you and 90% how you react to it!" And the way I heard it was like this:

"What happens to you isn't nearly as important as how you react to it!" (Author Unknown)

How Can This Help You?

Maybe you are at a dead end with your current job, sometimes we are forced to make the leap and do something different, do something on our own. Often times it takes a crisis to force us to start our own business, to change careers, or to make a life-changing decision that really needs to be made!

Remember, when things don't go as planned in your life, maybe, you're on the wrong pathway! Life isn't made up of things continuously going the right way or your way, sometimes there are bumps in the road! Sometimes your idea is not God's way; He might have a whole different pathway that He'd like to take you on!

That's why the front windshield in your car is so large, and the rearview mirror is small. There is so much more to see when you are looking ahead! The Bible talks about putting your hand to the plow. Jesus tells us that once we put our hand to the plow to never look back. Very few people in this day and age appreciate Jesus' use of the plow as an illustration of a life dedicated to the Lord. Think about it, the plow is shaped with a single steel blade attached to two wooden handles. A mule did most of the work by pulling the apparatus forward, but the farmer held on to direct the pathway of the blade. I dare you to try just one time an old-fashioned farmer's plow, and you'll quickly discover that using it is no easy task! This simple apparatus will bump and jerk your hands and arms, as it tears up the ground. There is only one way to make a straight line, and that is to stay focused on the work and keep your eyes forward every single second.

Discouragement sometimes forces us to look back at situations that should have been, could have been, and wishes that would have been. Don't look over your shoulder and dwell on your past regrets! Give up whatever draws your attention away from the task at hand!

"No one who puts a hand to the plow and looks back is fit for service in the kingdom of God." (Luke 9:62)

Chapter 10

I WOULD HAVE NAMED HER GRACE

The telephone rings at my gas station and I answer, "Hello, how may I help you?" "Honey, our baby was born this morning!" It was time to go see the baby we created and face the sudden reality of fatherhood. I take off in my VW. It's a hot August day as my Volkswagen makes it way from town. I traveled north over the mountains to the top of the state, a few hours away—about a hundred and some miles away. I arrive at the hospital about midday to meet Jennifer, the mother of the child I fathered.

She had spent most of the late spring covering up her pregnancy with large sweatshirts—trying to hide her tummy from the town folk until summer when she was to take up residence at a home for unwed mothers. She was allowed no contact with me after strict orders from her mother and father. It was determined, back in February or March when we announced the pregnancy to her parents, that they had better things in mind for her future than to spend it with a high school dropout like me.

Mom and dad had big plans for their captain of the swim team, high school prom queen, and Valedictorian; and I wasn't going to be any part of that equation. I had no part in any of the decision to have the baby put up for adoption, marriage, or any of that stuff. I was however informed—almost immediately—that I would be paying for all the necessary hospital bills concerning the unexpected arrival of our illegitimate child!

As I drove through the mountains, I felt very strange. Who knows what her, or the baby's, or my future holds at this juncture of our lives.

There are about 12–15 substantial limestone steps at the front of the hospital. As I look upward to the entrance of this old health institution I can feel the sweat drip down my back from the heat of the day. I'm excited, and so nervous—scared out of my mind. There's no way a 18 or 19-year-old should be going through these experiences. Yes, the sex was one thing we knew little about, but now childbirth, which we knew even less about. How does this happen?

And then, there is the new young mother, much younger than her years: a young woman who has a bright future as a professional artist at one of the most prominent art schools in the country. She should never have to go through this kind of experience without someone she can count on. Life isn't intended to be like this. Her parents were not here to support her; they were never going to be any part of this, and frankly, I wasn't being much support either. I lean over the front desk and check in with the nurses, and I am immediately shuffled off to see her by one of the nearby orderlies.

As I arrived at her humble little room, I could see that she was anticipating my arrival as she was already out of bed with her pajamas and robe on, and hair combed. She looked like she was never pregnant and hadn't given birth to a baby girl just literally hours before. We exchanged pleasantries and hugged like a brother would hug his sister—not like a husband and wife or lovers would embrace each other. I know now, but I didn't know then, the magical gift of birth and parenthood and that unadulterated fulfillment of those first few hours and days of a newly born baby's life. I was missing that incredible God-given joy.

"Isn't it wonderful?" I said quietly as we stood with other new parents looking through the glass at the rows of babies in bassinets. (I was afraid to say otherwise.) It did sound very awkward at the time, even with the commotion of how amazing an experience it was from everyone around us. The midwife started barking through the window, pointing at the tiny crib in which our baby lay fast asleep. Then a nurse picked her up and brought her to the window to show her off to her new, confused, young parents. There were weeping, over-joyed couples all around us looking at their newly born bundles of creation, while she and I were there to talk about keeping the baby or putting her up for adoption.

I've learned that bonding is essential for a child's survival, as I see it every day now with all the children that are brought into the world from loving conventional parents. And then the flip side of the coin from people who never have any intentions of getting married, but procreating, having children, moving in together, thinking they can live happily ever after! The biological capacity to bond and form attachments is genetically determined. The drive to survive is primary in all species. Infants are defenseless and must depend on a caring adult for survival, and our child wasn't going to have it from us, but from an adopted parent.

Bonding and attachment are terms that describe the affectional relationships between parents and their baby, and ours was destined to fail from the start. Pre-marital sex, a child, child parents, and top it off with her parents thinking that I'm wrong for their daughter. And as I think about it, what parent doesn't want the best for their daughter?

It was a short visit, and I left only a few hours after arriving. She and I decided to call it quits that day and give this glorious gift of creation, this little bundle of pure joy up for adoption, and leave her behind for someone with more responsibility.

She was already enrolled for fall classes at one of the most prestigious art schools. It didn't take long until we would regularly be speaking on the telephone, and I quickly responded by making trips to see her on the weekends.

I have learned long distance relationships usually never last because one person or the other will lose interest over time due to the space and time in between—that happened to be me. I know for a fact she was committed to finishing her education and getting her art degree, but I was a wreck waiting to happen. Here I am without church or Christ in my life, plus trying to make a gas station go, going out after work to the bars, getting in late and up early to repeat. She needed and deserved to be with a man, not me, she deserved so much more than I could or was willing to give her at the time.

All the while we were sneaking around behind her parents back, she even went so far as to spend the day riding on a bus from college to come and visit, so we could spend the weekend together. It was a big surprise to me when she showed up at my work. I blew her off and told her she should have called me as I had prior plans. That was the end of our relationship, and rightly so, only a genuinely delusional person would have stuck around for more embarrassment and punishment from a crappy boy-friend like me. Deep down inside she was healthier than that, and she knew she deserved better than I was giving her.

A Call From the Past—
What I Meant to Say Was…

Many years had gone by—nearly 20 years had come and gone, and she was still in my thoughts occasionally. But, equally on my mind was this 20-year-old daughter who was out there somewhere without an inkling of who was her mother or father. I had finally come to a point in my life with a lot of business and financial success and was often curious if either of them ever had thoughts of me.

More years flew by, and I finally tracked down her mother and mustered up the courage to call her. It was very uncomfortable, but I told her that I was sorry for all the pain and anguish I had put her and her husband through many years before. Even though by this time in my life, I was used to addressing rooms full of people, I was darn scared! The memory of how she always had a way of making me feel inferior to her or demeaned me when I was around her came to mind. I asked her at the time if she wouldn't mind helping me contact her daughter. She replied, "What would you like?" I responded, "Would you have your daughter call me someday? I would like to apologize for all the hurt and pain I caused her." She said, "Yes!" We said our goodbyes and ended that strange phone call. A couple of months went by, my desk phone rang in my office... and it was her! I never recognized her name until she said her maiden name and repeated her first name again.

The conversation didn't take long, but I remembered crying on the phone to her and telling her how sick to my stomach I was and how convicted I was over how I mistreated her. Most importantly, how I left her holding the bag with something as serious as a newborn child. She expressed to me that it was okay and that she had moved on and never looked back. She also said that our child was in her past, that her children and her husband never knew anything about it, and that was the way she wanted to keep it.

How Can This Help You?

A Charles Dickens quote:

"Reflect upon your blessings, of which every man has plenty; not on your past misfortunes, of which all men have some."

There were a couple of things that prompted my wanting to get in touch with her. On the one hand, I thought that I should allow sleeping dogs to lie and not to re-open that old wound for her. But my conscience was working on me since I had come to know Christ and I felt like I should share my heartfelt feelings. The second reason was that a couple of years before I contacted her mother I had a chance encounter with her. I was at a shopping center with my wife and my two daughters when I noticed her with her two teenage daughters. We met eye to eye and clearly spotted each other and knew immediately who the other one was. I felt like I had to tell her how happy I was for her and for the life she had made for herself.

While contacting her many years ago has helped me make restitution with her, I can tell you not a day goes by without me spotting a gal on the street, wondering if that could be my daughter and wanting or expecting a knock at my door from my daughter, saying, "Hello, my name is Grace!"

Have you ever done something in the past that you regret? Bring it to Jesus at the foot of the cross and give it to him. Receive His forgiveness and forgive yourself. Remember as long as you have breath, it is never too late to go back and speak to the person or people you've hurt or offended and make restitution.

"But in keeping with his promise, we are looking forward to a new heaven and a new earth, where righteousness dwells. So then, dear friends, since you are looking forward to this, make every effort to be found spotless, blameless and at peace with him." (2 Peter 3:13-14)

Chapter 11

NOTHING HAPPENS
IN THE WORLD UNTIL
SOMETHING IS SOLD!

The phone rings loudly from the nightstand—not far from my head. In my stupor of sleep depravity and my unconscious state from another late night at my body shop, I pick up the receiver, "Hello?" "Good morning, its Karl from the Chevy store! Did I wake you?" "No, no. Go ahead. What's up?" I figured he was calling about a car I was painting for him. At the time, I was doing a lot of custom painting, striping, and things like that for the Chevrolet dealership; and I thought he was calling about a car I was working on for the dealership.

As it turned out, a couple of weeks before this phone call, Karl and Alex, the General Sales Manager, popped the question to me and asked if I ever thought about selling cars. Trying to persuade me of a better life they asked, "Aren't you tired of all that sanding dust and breathing paint fumes all day? We think you would make a great salesperson at the dealership, and if you were open to it, we would like to test your sales ability!"

Karl's comment on the phone that morning was "We received your test results back, and we would like to talk to you about selling cars for us. When would it be convenient to come to the dealership to chat about a possible career in auto sales?" I admit I was kind of stunned. After all, I was still trying to coax myself awake and a little mystified; but I didn't allow my excitement to take over. I replied, "When would you like to see me?" My time was somewhat flexible since I was self-employed, with only one or two employees. Karl's comment was, "Why don't you come and see us now?" "Okay, I can be there in about an hour, would that work for you?", I replied. "Sure, if you can be here in an hour that would be great!"

I jumped from the bed and immediately called my mother. She was the baker at the local hotel. She was very excited for me and wished me well. I was quickly thinking, "Wow, a salary, a new car, and gasoline for my demonstrator. This is going to be awesome!" I ran to fill the tub with hot water, hopped in, shaved, and put on the only suit and necktie that I owned. A little tight, since it was several years old, but the clear plaid gray suit was still quite stylish, albeit the pants a tad short, but no one would ever notice if I would hang them on my hips.

I loved automobiles. My brother spoon-fed me motor oil from the time I was old enough to visit his hotrod garage! I had just finished my Corvette paint job, so when I pulled into the dealership, I felt confident, trying to look the part of a new sales applicant at the Chevrolet Cadillac store in town. Arriving right on time, I went to the receptionist and asked for Karl and Alex. Karl came in from one direction of the dealership and Alex from another. They greeted me from both sides with firm handshakes and enthusiastic smiles. We went into Alex's office where I'd been many times before since I'd done loads of particular paint jobs for them over the past couple of years.

It seemed Karl was the talker of the two of them; he held a manila folder which contained the sales test I had taken a couple of weeks back. It was a sales aptitude test with a predictor of sales ability. He said, "Well, your test results came back very positive. Both Alex and I thought that would be the case all along. We would like to offer you a job selling cars for us!"

My first thought was, "Wow, unbelievable!' One of my good friends was a sales guy at the dealership, and he was very influential in a lot of the work that I received from them. Although he was only a few years older than I was, he was very successful, a great looking guy, always dressed very sharp and well groomed. The women loved him, and he was quite well liked by the dealer owner. He seemed to have it made. He was a favorite of everyone he came in contact with. My thoughts were, "Wow, I hope, I can be accepted and liked as well as him!"

Alex and Karl quickly put the pitch on me and got into all the possibilities of me working there—advancement, sales achievement awards, big commission checks, sales incentive trips, and so on. Needless to say, I had to pinch myself! I asked, "So, what's the starting salary?" Then, the shoe dropped as Alex stepped in and said, "Oh, it's a draw, not a salary." I had no idea what a draw was, but I was about to find out. He continued, "You will be 100% commission, but each week you get a draw check that comes out of your month end commissions." "How much is that?" I asked. Karl interjected, "It is $65 a week." Sixty-five dollars a week, I thought, "That's only about $1.60 an hour—for crying out loud that's minimum wage! Waitresses make more minimum wage than that, that's less than 10% an hour compared to what I am making now!" I said to them, "Let me get this straight. You don't pay me anything unless I sell something?" And they replied, "Yep! But, guys like some of our most experienced salespeople make a lot of money. They have a huge clientele built up with quite a sales following." At the time, I had no idea what a lot of money was; but I knew deep down inside I didn't want to paint cars, be a body & fender man, or for that fact, work in a machine shop the rest of my life. I even liked the sound of, "Hi, I sell new Chevrolets and Cadillacs for a living!" Wow, that sounded so classy! I told them I would take the job and asked, "When do I start?" "You have several weeks of product training we want you to learn, and then the first of next month we'll put you into the floor schedule," Karl stated with an outstretched hand. I shook it, and Alex's, too and sealed the deal.

Here I was; a high school dropout with a G.E.D. diploma and I thought, this is a great opportunity. I kept my body shop for about a year or so after that, working evenings and mornings when I didn't have to go in until 3:00 PM. But every morning, I had to be at the dealership for a 9:00 AM sales meeting. I had to be dressed for the sales meeting, so I would have to get up, clean-up, get suited up, and head to the meeting; and then go to my body shop and work until 2:00 PM, shower again, and go work at the dealership until 9:00 PM. Most nights, I would go to the body shop and work until midnight or 1:00 AM, and then go for drink at the local watering hole (oh, and by the way, I was lying about my age to get served beer) and then head home and do the same thing all over again the next day. After a year or so of this pattern, it took quite a toll on me. I was doing okay selling cars, and I was doing ok at the shop, and the time came to pick one or the other, so I chose the automobile business and closed the body shop.

The longer I was in the car business I knew I didn't want to be part of the 80/20 rule. If you're not familiar with that, it is: 80% of the salespeople are selling only 20% of the merchandise. This doesn't just pertain to automobile sales, it can be selling anything. My first year or so, I think, I averaged about 13 or 14 cars a month, which was about the upper middle of the sales team. I would call it later in life, "The cream of the crap, or the best of the middle!"

I became a voracious reader, reading everything I could get my hands on concerning sales, how to sell, and success. The dealership knew I loved the business by that time, they would send me to Chevrolet's selling school that was nearby and the results paid off. The rest of the salesmen had no interest in school or classes on how to sell or how to be better themselves. But I had one thing in mind, and that was being the best and one day soon being a sales manager. I was consistently one, two or three in car sales and in no time, I was yearning for a sales manager position. But, at 21 or 22-years-old, I think the dealer/operator had a problem with that. Soon, I left the Chevy store and took a General Sales Manager's position at another dealership in town.

Selling cars and being a commissioned salesperson can be a lot like life itself. You really only get out of it what you put into it! We all need self-discipline. No one else is responsible for your success or your failure—just you. I always loved this verse for a situation like this.

> *"Do you not know that in a race all the runners run, but only one gets the prize? Run in such a way as to get the prize. Everyone who competes in the games goes into strict training. They do it to get a crown that will not last, but we do it to get a crown that will last forever."* (I Corinthians 9:24- 25)

One thing was for sure, I had a gift!

I love America; I love the fact that everyone has the same chance of excellence as I do. Everyone puts their pants on the same way—one leg at a time—they are no different than I am. America is indeed the land of opportunity. People who really want to make it in life come to this country for freedom and opportunity and a lot of times with nothing but the shirt on their backs. Most make a good living for themselves because they work hard, and they know the meaning of never quitting. My father was that way when he came to America as a stowaway on a Greek Freighter, without as much as a dime in his pocket and the clothes on his back. Millions of others have done it the same way.

The bottom line is: I was given an opportunity to be someone better than what I had been. I was given a chance by someone to excel at something with a future, a big future!

ONE GOOD TURN DESERVES ANOTHER! WHAT I MEANT TO SAY WAS...

It's funny how things work out in life. It's a story that I'm sure most of us have one or two just like it. Several years later, I had become the General Sales Manager at the very same auto dealership where Alex and Karl had hired me, but under a different name and a new owner. The dealership was doing incredibly well. I was able to escalate the sales from about 40 cars per month to consistently over 200 vehicles per month. In the meantime, Karl, the sales manager who originally had hired me in the business, had left the Chevrolet Cadillac store after a few years and started his own used car dealership. During some pretty tough financial times, a few years later Karl did some things I know he mainly regretted later. I knew the deep down core of Karl: he was a fair and confident man of integrity. I hired him as a salesman, and literally, a few months later I made him my used car manager. It turned out to be a tremendously profitable decision for me and the dealership and a break for Karl.

As far as Alex was concerned, Alex had retired but was way too active to sit around and count his money and eat bonbons all day. I hired Alex as a salesperson; it was unique and a genuine hoot to work side-by-side with two of my mentors. I have always owed a high debt of gratitude to both of them. They saw something in me that no one had seen before, and I've never forgotten that!

Just on a side note: When I applied for the mechanic's job at the Chevrolet store many years before, there had been a service manager. When I returned to manage the original dealership's post-successor, that same person was still employed as the service manager. He remembered that he turned me down as an applicant as a mechanic. He asked me that day if that would have any bearing on him working under me as the service manager. I assured him it didn't matter and that we all need experience before we are presented with the task at hand. I told him I had not been ready at that time to be a line mechanic, and that God had something different in store for me. I appreciated him, and neither of us ever made mention of it ever again,

How Can This Help You?

"There is a time for everything, and a season for every activity under the heavens: a time to be born and a time to die, a time to plant, and a time to plant and a time to uproot, a time to kill and a time to heal, a time to tear down and a time to build, a time to weep and a time to laugh, a time to mourn and a time to dance, a time to scatter stones and a time to gather them, a time to embrace and a time to refrain from embracing." (Ecclesiastes 3: 1–5)

For me, this was the time to repay a favor and remember someone who helped me in a time of need. Sooner or later, what goes around comes around, both positive and negative situations... choose wisely!

Chapter 12

GETTING RIGHT WITH GOD

My car is pulled alongside the road, headlights on, motor running; my head bowed in prayer, begging God to change my heart as tears run down my cheeks.

By this point in my life, I have two beautiful, healthy little girls one that is three-years-old, and the other one a year and a half old, along with a wife of five years. My marriage to this point has been a total lie to my wife, and I know it is time to do something different with my life. I am a total wreck! I certainly don't want my daughters to grow up to be a poser like I was—I wanted them to be raised in a spiritual environment, with accountability. I always had church in my life. I sang in the men and boys' choir for years, but being that close to the preaching every Sunday morning didn't make me any holier. Frankly, I don't think I really understood the significance of a personal relationship with Christ. Oh, I was confirmed as a Christian when I was about 10 years old, and then I could take Communion. It felt so ritualistic, and I thought that Communion was just an act and not for honoring Jesus Christ for His death and resurrection at Calvary.

You would think I should be happy with my life. After all, I have two healthy kids, a new house that's practically paid for, and really no financial debt of any kind. We have ample home-owner's and health insurance, and to top it off two brand new company cars provided by my employer with gasoline and insurance included. But if I've learned anything in life, it's things don't make you happy. Oh, sometimes they glaze over the crux of the matter at hand and make you smile every now and then because you can buy something expensive or go out for a good dinner more often than most. But, money doesn't really make you happy, only you can make you happy!

In January, we started attending a fundamental Bible church that I was introduced to by my older brother. He was a head over heels Christian and talked to everyone about his newfound faith, Christianity, and salvation. I knew from the moment that I stepped foot in the front door that sooner or later there was going to be a day of reckoning with my life. I didn't want it, but I had a feeling I wasn't going to have any choice in the matter. I knew it had to happen and I had no control over when or how I just had to come clean with my life one day soon.

I told my brother when he first invited us to church on that cold January Sunday morning, "The first guy that steps out of the pews, and into the isles and starts waving his hands and praising and shouting Jesus... I'm out of here!" After all, I grew up in a traditional Protestant church in a small town. It was always very formal and none of this AMEN stuff! Let's face it; you don't go through the confession process like in a Catholic church. You have the—let us pray, now stand, no, it is time to sit, and finally kneel. Don't all you Catholics, Lutherans, or Episcopalians get mad, it's true? The church is just way formal compared to a fundamental Bible-believing church, where the only focus is Salvation and Jesus.

As each day passed, my burden to be right or get right with God grew stronger. My language was starting to change, the way I treated people changed, even the amount of money I put in the offering plate changed every week. I was quickly learning about being a new creation without realizing that I wasn't changing a thing. I also realized that you can't out give God!

It's the middle of May, and I'm on my way home after a typical 12-hour shift at the car dealership. I'm praying to God about my convictions and my sinful life. I could no longer live with myself. With tears rushing down my cheeks; both of my hands gripped the steering wheel with a death grip. Finally, I have to pull over alongside the road. I can't see from my eyes since they are filled with tears. I am trembling as I cry out to Jesus to save my life from further destruction. It's dark outside. I put my four-way flashers on and continue to pray for forgiveness, and I invite Christ into my life, to live in my heart, and wash my sins whiter than snow. I begged to have His blood cleanse me from my sins and save me from my wickedness and change my life. "Oh, God!" I cried out loud. I had no idea what to pray, but I knew it was time to get serious about a life with Christ in it. I was an evil person, with no ability to stop the evilness myself. On the surface, I looked perfect: the nice suit and necktie, two well-dressed kids, a couple of new cars, a good job, but my life on the inside was a dirty, hidden bag of sinful desires!

I soon learned that I had no choice in the matter from the book of John:

"You did not choose me, but I chose you and appointed you so that you might go and bear fruit—fruit that will last—

and so that whatever you ask in my name the Father will give you." (John 15:16)

This is the way the grace of God begins, it is a constraint that we can never escape, we can only obey it! God does not ask us to do the things that are naturally easy for us. He just asks us to do the things that we are perfectly fit to do through His grace, and that is where the cross we must bear will always come in.

It was a hard ride home. When I walked through the door, I didn't share my experience with my wife, because I felt the Holy Spirit was working hard on my heart, and I knew I had to come clean with my sins from there on. I knew that I had not only to confess all my sins to God, but to come clean with my life, with my wife as well, and then make it right with the relationships that I had been destroying around me.

I was sickened when I thought about all my wrongs—people that I had affected betrayed and lied to, and very quickly, I realized this.

"You, God, are my God, earnestly I seek you; I thirst for you, my whole being longs for you, in a dry and parched land where there is no water. I have seen you in the sanctuary and beheld your power and your glory. Because your love is better than life, my lips will glorify you. I will praise you as long as I live, and in your name, I will lift up my hands. I will be fully satisfied as with the richest of foods; with singing lips, my mouth will praise you. On my bed I remember you; I think of you through the watches of the night. Because you are my help, I sing in the shadow of your wings. I cling to you; your right hand upholds me." (Psalm 63:1-6)

Making it Right— What I Meant to Say Was...

Let me start by saying that the consequences are much easier to live with before you commit to the sin—the guilt would be nil! Unfortunately, you commit stupid things, and then you have to go back and repave roads, mend fences all over the place that you ripped up in your path to destruction. Trust me, God is there with His Holy Spirit tugging on our heartstrings even before we get into a sinful lifestyle. We are all born with a sinful nature, but, it is what we do with it that matters. There is a conviction side in our lives that is available to us if we would only get out of the way and listen to God speak it to us! I knew it was wrong to commit adultery, to have an affair with someone else's wife. I have heard the commandment that says, "Thou shall not covet thy neighbor's wife!" I had lived my life to this point filled with fornication, pre-marital sex, affairs, adultery, and now it was time to pay the piper and make it right with everyone!

How Can This Help You?

I was lucky enough to make a positive decision in my life to accept Jesus Christ as my Savior. My choices in life to this point hadn't been that good, but at least I made the decision to allow God to change my life. The only way I could change the deep-seated path of sin in my life was to ask for help. I wasn't capable of doing it myself.

Drugs, theft, pornography, sex addiction, alcoholism, murder, or any other sin are measured the same way. Sin is sin no matter if you stole a quart of milk at the corner grocery store or murdered someone. God looks at it all the same way.

What is so totally cool to me about all of this is: I didn't have one, two, or even three affairs (that's not the cool part, the cool part is), it speaks in the Bible about 70 times seven, and it is synonymous with God's eternal forgiveness.

"Then Peter came to Jesus and asked, 'Lord, how many times shall I forgive my brother or sister who sins against me? Up to seven times,' Jesus answered, 'I tell you, not seven times, but seventy times seven times.'" (Matthew 18:21-22)

Jesus isn't telling us to forgive our brothers 490 times, or 70 times, or 77 times. He's telling us we should always forgive our brothers when they have sinned against us. God in heaven has forgiven us all of humanity's sins. How wrong it would be for us to deny our brothers and sisters similar forgiveness for much lesser matters. Back in the book of Matthew, Jesus describes this parable:

"Therefore, the kingdom of heaven is like a king who wanted to settle accounts with his servants. As he began the settlement, a man who owed him ten thousand talents was brought to him. Since he was not able to pay, the master ordered that he and his wife and his children and all that he had be sold to repay the debt. The servant fell on his knees before him. 'Be patient with me,' he begged, 'and I will pay back everything.' The servant's master took pity on him, canceled the debt and let him go.

But when that servant went out, he found one of his fellow servants who owed him a hundred denarii. He grabbed him and began to choke him. 'Pay back what you owe me!' he demanded. His fellow servant fell to his knees and begged him, 'Be patient with me, and I will pay you back.' But he refused. Instead, he went off and had the man thrown into prison until he could pay the debt.

When the other servants saw what had happened, they were greatly distressed and went and told their master everything that had happened. Then the master called the servant in. 'You wicked servant,' he said, 'I canceled all that debt of yours because you begged me to. Shouldn't you have had mercy on your fellow servant just as I had on you?' In anger, his master turned him over to the jailers to be tortured, until he should pay back all he owed. This is how my heavenly Father will treat each of us, unless we forgive our brother from our heart." (Matthew 18:23-35)

Chapter 13

THE FUNERAL

I'm sitting at the seafood restaurant in the local mall with a few of my salesmen buddies and the owner of the car dealership I managed. They are tipping their drinks to me, making a toast to my newborn daughter after her birth early that morning.

I glanced across the horseshoe-shaped bar, and I see an old friend—an ex-girlfriend from many years past. She ended up pregnant from me and would bare a son from a brief sexual encounter that happened about five years earlier. We said our uncomfortable hellos from across the bar. Finally, as my friends decided the party was over for them, they left. She found her way to my side of the bar and sat down beside me congratulating me on my new daughter. We chatted for a while and about the time she was ready to head out, she asked me if I would like to come to her house and see our sleeping son.

It was a very uncomfortable invitation. After all, my wife and newborn daughter were resting in the nearby hospital, and I was out for a celebratory drink. It was bad enough that I had gone for a celebratory drink, but to run into her for the first time in years was a bit overwhelming. Reluctantly, I decided I would swing by her house on my way home and meet my son for the first time.

By this time in my life, I had come to know Christ as my Savior. Furthermore, I was being trained to be a man of God, so I knew I could keep my past sexual advances in total check. I grabbed my sport coat from behind my bar stool and headed out for a quick trip to her home. We arrived moments later at her house a few miles away. I parked and headed inside. The babysitter quickly ducked out of the way, and she invited me upstairs to see this sleeping cherub. He was about three or four years old at the time, sleeping soundly, stretched out sideways in his bed, covers scattered everywhere. So peaceful, so beautiful was this handsome olive skinned dark haired little Italian–Albanian boy. Up until this point in my life, I had never met him. It was a joy, on the one hand, to see what we created, and a feeling of ashamedness on the other side that I had never been around to throw a ball or teach him to ride a bike. I think every father longs for a son of his own, but selfish circumstances prevented that in this case.

She had written to me on many occasions telling me of her pregnancy, but I was at a space in my life where I didn't accept the responsibility. I did, however, help with the payment of hospital birth bills and after he was born, she had made requests through domestic relations that I pay child support, which I gladly paid.

A few months had passed after the evening that I met that little guy. I received a letter from her attorney, informing me that she wanted me to give up any rights to the fatherhood of our child, and for her 100% rights to him, I would also be released from any future child support payments. Her comment was,

"You have a family of your own to raise now," and she added, "I am capable with a good paying job to support him on my own!" My wife and I spoke about it and thought that maybe it was a gift from her to me to be released, so I signed the agreement.

In years to come, my faith had been growing, and a stronger relationship with God had placed a burden on me that maybe I could make a difference in this young boy's life. I would call periodically to ask her if I could see him on occasion, but the answer was always no! That didn't stop me. My business career was thriving, and the thought of knowing I had a son without a father wasn't going away. Relentless calls would always lead to a "No" answer. Finally, one day, her boyfriend said, "Look, man, please quit calling us! She's not interested in hearing from you and her son thinks you're dead!"

My children were nearing adulthood and were about to graduate from high school. Within a period of about four or five months, I would see our caller ID that our home phone number had been receiving calls from my son's home phone number. Puzzled at first, but, after months of hang-ups, I hoped that my son had finally wanted to make contact with me. After days of contemplating calling him, I mustered up the courage and decided to call the phone number. She answered the phone, she knew it was me immediately. When she heard my voice, and I asked to speak to our son—he was 23 years old at the time—her response was, "He is old enough to make his own decisions!" Then she proceeded to ask him if he wanted to speak to me. His response was "Yes!" We chatted on the phone for a while and then decided we would meet for coffee later that night in town.

Over the years, before we finally began our relationship, I would see him running around town here and there riding his bike, or on occasions at an afternoon swim at the local swimming pool. So, I knew he was a healthy and an active, good looking boy.

When I met him—the same day as my phone call—it was like looking at myself in the mirror some 20 years earlier. His arms had the same kind of dark arm hair that my arms had, his hands looked like a duplicate mold of my hands. Height, weight, color, and features revealed there was no denying this dark brown haired, brown eyed, handsome young man was my son! He carried a swagger of confidence as he walked to meet me and a smile that would make anyone melt at his feet. We shook hands and exchanged a friendly guy hug. We sat down and talked for three hours about our lives.

He would quickly become a part of our family, and his two new sisters adopted him just like he was the big brother they had always heard about. Summer picnics, trips to the malt shop frequently happened, along with evening family dinners, and seeing my son was a daily occurrence.

In the meantime, my wife and I had purchased a building downtown. We were in the middle of a complete renovation and makeover for a Salon & Day Spa. My son was employed doing used car reconditioning, and we thought it was in everyone's best interest for him to come to work for us helping our general contractor do the remodel of her salon. Our general contractor and my son hit it off well and worked hard on the project side-by-side, all summer long and well into the fall. I was pretty handy with a paintbrush and roller, so when it came time for the interior painting, my son and I would sling paint for hours on end. Between buckets of paint and hot pizza, we would have deep conversations about life, Christianity, and eternal life.

Our talks were a sharing time for us. I soon learned he was a young father himself to an infant daughter and also that he had never met her as well. Not by age but of maturity, he was no more ready or responsible for fatherhood than I was at age 18. He was much older than I was at his age. Hearing about him being a father hurt my heart, knowing that he probably followed in my foolish footsteps. I was never there to guide him through the tight spots of early manhood just like my father was not around for my much-needed direction. My son was head over heels in love with a gal locally, but they had a tumultuous relationship that was on and off quite frequently. As we would sling paint, I would hear over and over again how sexual their relationship was. I repeated to him that sex between him and his girlfriend was their business and something that he should never share with anyone, especially me! "It's between you and her and no one else, period!"

The more I heard about their love affair, the more it reminded me of my former life. His girlfriend's father wanted more for his only daughter then he was capable of giving her, and she was warned continuously to break off the relationship between the two of them, and finish college. They were together, and then apart, and they repeated this cycle quite often. Finally, just after Christmas, she informed him it was over for good. That crushed my son and pushed him into a deep, dark depression.

He was without a driver's license, so I would pick him up for work and drop him off practically every night. It was Friday night, and he asked me to drop him off at the tavern just down the street from his house. I was apprehensive, but he assured me he was okay and was meeting some friends and was going to blow some steam off. Our deadline for opening my wife's salon was nearing, and there was plenty of finish work to be done. When I dropped him off that evening, I told him I would pick him up promptly at 9:00 AM the next morning.

I was at his house just like I said I would be, but he was a no-show! His mother said, "He didn't come home last night; maybe, he stayed with his girlfriend!" I didn't have access to her phone number, so I had no way of getting a hold of her. My son had a garage nearby his mother's house that he worked in occasionally on a Fiat Convertible that he owned. So, I circled by his garage that morning, but there was no sign of him there either.

I made phone calls on and off all day long to his mother's house, but no answer. That evening passed quickly, and my suspicions that something was seriously wrong were growing faster by the minute. Sunday morning and all-day Sunday proved to be a dead-end with all my phone calls trying to track down his whereabouts.

Finally, I received a call from his mother on Monday. "Bill?" She said shakily. "Yes," I replied. "We found my son late last night! He hung himself in his garage! I went over to his garage late last night and discovered him!" My heart sank as I heard the silence on the phone. I said, "I will be over right away!" She said, "Don't bother. It's my problem, not yours! You have no business in this matter!" I yelled back, "He was my son too!" I hung up the phone and immediately drove over to her house, but it was not a comfortable situation. After giving my condolences, I left. I felt as though she blamed his suicide on me. And frankly, I felt like if I had been involved in his life sooner than I was, I could have prevented his untimely death.

Our family prepared for the funeral. I had never been to a funeral of someone who had committed suicide, let alone my own child. It was administered by a Catholic priest, and frankly, I don't think he was sure that my son would be at eternal rest because of his taking his own life. It was an awful service attended by friends and family from far and wide. His mother came from a large Italian family of boys, and she was the only girl. I sat in the back of the church supported by my family. Feeling as though I should not be there just by the comments and looks that I received by the family. After the service, she announced that after the trip to the cemetery and burial she wanted everyone to come back to the house and eat. Everyone, but me! As I passed her going out of the church giving my condolences, she made it quite explicit that I was not to come to the house under any circumstances.

GENERATIONAL SINS— WHAT I MEANT TO SAY WAS...

I think this is every parent's worst nightmare. There are probably only a couple of things worse than losing a child by suicide, and that would be missing a child through abduction. Having to go to your child's funeral, maybe the most painful thing I ever had to face. Why? I had to deal with the birth of an illegitimate son this time ending in suicide! A parent dealing with the depth of grief concerning a child lost to suicide is considered the worst possible grief ever!

His mother and I only had a few dates at most, but after a fun-filled day at the amusement park, we ended up in bed, and a son was the result of that encounter. To this day, I remember that haunting moment in the heat of passion, and as those sensual words were exchanged back and forth during that evening, I had no idea what I was wishing for!

Be careful what you wish for in the thralls of a heated sexual relationship! Sometimes, when you make a statement, God will fulfill what you ask for! Sometimes we ask for things that we really don't want!

When will we realize the results of our sins have such a lasting effect, not only for our generation but for generations to come! Look at my son's daughter, and my granddaughter, who has no idea of who I am. It's all a direct result of my sin from many years earlier. How horrible is that knowing I have another child out there knowing she has a grandfather and I can't reach out to her?

Oh, Father, God, please forgive me for being such a coward and for all the lives I have wrecked with my selfishness. Forgive me for the loneliness and sleepless nights that I caused his mother while going through her pregnancy, alone. Forgive me for the nights that she had to take care of a sick son, and all the hardships of single parenthood. And most of all, God, please forgive me for her losing her only son at such a young age!

I know now she has to have feelings of guilt, anger, abandonment, and denial. I know she must feel numb, and like most parents, would think that she failed as a mother. How do I know that? Because I only knew him for a short time and those were the feelings I had, and for that, I am beyond sorry! As an absent father having feelings for him, I can only imagine how deeply she loved her only son.

How Can This Help You?

Somehow or another, I have learned to have an unstoppable determination for His Holiness. But that hasn't been without more trips up and down the ladder than I care to remember. There have been many times in my life, where if it weren't for my faith in God, I probably would have taken my own life! Of course, when I had thought of desperation, I've always thought of the wreckage that it leaves behind, with parents, spouses, children, and even friends, and for myself, I could not be that cowardly.

I think, it takes a strong person, on the one hand, and a weak person on the other, to commit suicide, and I am not sure which it is. But through the hope of eternal life, I choose to live for Him, albeit, not perfectly most of the time, but to live! Surrender your will to Jesus unconditionally and irrevocably to live and make a difference!

Philippians says this:

"I eagerly expect and hope that I will in no way be ashamed, but will have sufficient courage so that now as always Christ will be exalted in my body, whether by life or by death." (Philippians 1:20)

And then in verse 21 it goes on to say:

"For to me, to live is Christ and to die is gain." (Philippians 1:21)

Whether it means life or death—it makes no difference!

Oswald Chambers says:

"Before we choose to follow God's will, a crisis must develop in our lives!"

I know most of my life I have had those gentler nudges that Chambers touches on, but I chose to ignore them, not once, not twice but many times until I had to experience a crisis.

Don't do what I did. Listen to the nudges and live your life for Christ!

Chapter 14

A CHEERFUL GIVER

I'm standing in the hallway of my recreation room and the telephone rings, "Hello?" "Is Bill there?" "Yes, this is Bill." "Bill, this is Judge Jack Wayne from the church." "Hello, your Honor!" I have known Judge Jack most of my life. Jack was one of the senior members in the men and boys' choir at the church that I sang in and attended since I had been a child. I always had a significant amount of respect for the Judge. Although I always addressed him as "Your Honor," he was never pontificating, pompous, or aloof. Jack was Jack. A kind-hearted fair and very humble man.

I am not sure how long after I was saved that I learned how to give generously. It indeed wasn't that night on the telephone. Jack was calling members of the church, asking for pledges for their annual fund drive. He said, "Billy, you are old enough to be regularly giving at the church, and we would like to get you included in our pledge drive." He continued, "How much could I count on you for? Would $50 be affordable?" I know at this time Jack was referring to $50 a week, but at the time, I thought he was referring to $50 a year. My comment was, "Sure, I can give you $50 for the year!"

Within a few months of that, I found myself attending a fundamental Bible church quite regularly. The more I gave, the more I earned, and I never gave because I thought there was a formulation for giving. But as I think of it now, I believe there is; you give 10 percent of your earnings, and God heaps it back to you 10 times over that—at least that's what it seemed like to me!

I'll never forget a camping trip I went on with some of my lifelong friends who are devout Christians. We went to the campground service that Sunday morning, and at the end of the service, the fellow preaching the message passed around his hat for donations. I generously placed a $5 bill in the hat and when my buddy opened up his wallet his girlfriend dove into his pile of bills like it was a shopping spree and pulled out a $50 bill. I knew I was making a lot more money than he was, but his giving heavily influenced me at how much money he so willingly and freely offered to that preacher. He didn't know the guy from Adam, and yet he gave so cheerfully and generously. I was so impressed with that episode. It started a lot of thinking in my head in regards to my cheap spirituality.

When I first starting attending the fundamental church, I remember the plate coming around and the first week I put in a $10 bill, the next week a $20 bill, the week after that a $50 bill, and soon I was giving more in a week than I had ever offered in a year. Things were starting to change big time in my life financially. I was working at a dead-from-the-neck-up Chrysler store struggling to make ends meet. All of a sudden; I received a great job offer with a starting salary at almost twice what I was currently making. But that wasn't all; my new employer was going to take care of all of my family health insurance, a pair of company cars with gasoline and not just one car for me but a fancy new Chevrolet for my wife as well!

In the first year, my income doubled, the next year it almost doubled again, and in a span of about five to six years, I was making well over $500,000 a year. The more money I made, the more I stuffed the offering plate with cash. Missionaries who had needs, this person, or that person who fell into tough circumstances were mysteriously given some help quietly. I had even gotten to the point—because I had access to automobiles— when a missionary would come home on leave, I would buy them an excellent inexpensive ride for their stay in the States. When they would leave for the field again, they would pass that vehicle on to the next person who needed it.

I guess God knew my heart better than I did, after all, He created me. God loves a cheerful giver, and I felt like it was one of my gifts in life to give abundantly. Healthy finances were a gift. God gave me the ability to earn money beyond anything I could have ever dreamed or conceived of, so I wanted to be a cheerful giver.

But the more money you make, the more independent a person can get. As it turned out, I was no different than anyone else in the world. I loved nice things including fancy boats—I loved boats! I purchased eight boats in seven years, each one bigger than the prior one. Each one with a matching tow vehicle and all the accessories—like matching life vests, lines, and towels to coordinate. We loved the beach. Who doesn't, right? So, we bought a beach house! We liked that one so much we bought the beach house aside of ours as an investment property. We had to dress the part we were playing, who wanted to be seen in everyday clothing? So, we were no longer buying clothing at Sears or J.C. Penny's, but at the most exclusive stores in the area. And we all loved shopping while on vacation. When we would go away, we would come home with bags of new clothing and even new suitcases to pack it in.

I remember one day my wife saying to me, "Aren't you ever happy with what you have? Don't you worry about what the neighbors think every time you bring home a bigger boat or bigger camper?" She went on to say, "You are embarrassing me, I don't know how to answer our friends! Must you always keep doing things bigger and better, and buying more and more all the time?" My answer was, "No, we earn it. It's none of their business how we spend it! I don't have to be accountable to them for my finances, we pay our bills on time, we give generously, and we have no debt to speak of!"

GOD WANTS YOUR HEART— WHAT I MEANT TO SAY WAS...

Wow, I was so stupid ever to think that God would place me on the earth solely for giving. I learned quickly that God doesn't want my money, He wants my heart! Remember that when you think you are irreplaceable in the God giving arena, God can raise an Army in minutes—probably seconds—to do what you are doing, and they'll do a better job! He can change the circumstances to no longer use you when you become unusable, and believe me, He will, and He did!

HOW CAN THIS HELP YOU?

At least with my giving, the right hand never knew what the left hand was doing.

"But when you give to the needy, do not let your left hand know what your right hand is doing." (Matthew 6:3)

Thank God for at least making me a cheerful giver and never broadcasting to the world, "Oh I did this, and I did that, or I gave this much to so and so!" Generosity is encouraged by Apostle Paul in 2 Corinthians. Remember this: When you are sitting in church and the pastor speaks about giving, do yourself a favor and give abundantly and give cheerfully!

"Whoever sows sparingly will also reap sparingly, and whoever sows generously will also reap generously. Each of you should give what you have decided in your heart to give, not reluctantly or under compulsion, for God loves a cheerful giver." (2 Corinthians 9:6-7)

From that time on, my heart cries to give to someone in need. I sometimes wonder if God will ever make me a giver like I once was? I hope so, and I know I will give differently without going to the candy store and buying everything I can feast my eyes on! There are many times when someone has a financial need, and I can do nothing about it, but pray and console them. Those are the times when my heart breaks to be a generous giver—for God loves a cheerful giver. As I have also learned God loves prayer warriors and that is quite a gift as well!

Chapter 15

I LOOKED UP AND SAW A SIGN!

I'm sitting big-chested and proud in my new Corvette in the parking lot of the Chevrolet dealership that I just purchased. I'm 35 years old, and I just left the settlement table with my wife where I laid down a $675,000 down-payment on a 2.9 million dollar purchase of an automobile dealership. I am sitting here in total amazement, overjoyed watching the man operate the crane changing the sign from the prior owner's name to my name. The thought rushes over me, "Thank you, Lord!" My prayers have all been answered. I was approved with Chevrolet and G.M.A.C., and the settlement could not have gone more smoothly. I can now operate my own Chevrolet dealership on my terms. This had been a dream for a long, long time—lots of planning, lots of schooling, then looking at dealerships all over the east coast. There was plenty of preparation, prayer, countless phone calls, and sleepless nights. Every dime I had available in cash, stocks, property sales, investments, and personal assets had gone into this venture. As I am watching the sign folks, this voice suddenly comes to me from my subconscious, "Bill, you are never going to make it!" It was like it was from a movie scene from *Field of Dreams*, when Kevin Costner heard, "If you build it, and they will come!"

I ignored the voice, thinking this can't be true. "God, why didn't you tell me this, 60 minutes earlier before I plopped down every penny I had to my name?" I immediately thought to myself, "Why would God place me in my own auto dealership, provide the approvals, and the down payment in a strong market, 100 miles from where I grew up just to have me fail?" The positive thinker in me suppressed this voice and muffled the sound by quickly diverting my attention elsewhere. We got out of our car and headed inside the dealership to introduce ourselves to all the employees, and to let them know that my wife and I were the new owners. We were ecstatic. We said our hellos, goodbyes, and headed to dinner with our attorney and his wife for a celebration of a year's tireless work. After all, this car dealership deal was dead and alive more times than a cat with nine lives. That should have been a clue right then and there! But lots of champagne, great food, laughs, and celebration was literally the calm before the storm. That night was probably the best night of sleep I would have for the next five or six years!

I watched the pieces starting to crumble quickly. One proverbial brick at a time was pulled from the foundation weakening my stance at the dealership every day. The dealership was located on the east end of town in a high-density low-income area. From the surface, it looked depressed, but I looked beyond that at all the opportunity and potential that the dealership had. It's funny how things happen and how things unwound so rapidly.

From a financial aspect, I personally earned about $525,000 that year, $375,000 from the dealership that I worked at and another $150,000 from my two-year-old advertising agency. I did my auto dealership financing through General Motors finance arm, known as Motors Holding (MH) Company. MH financed auto dealerships for qualified candidates of GM dealerships, which I was! I was Chevrolet's bright new shining star, breaking one sales record after another, taking the worst earned market penetration dealership in the country to 10th in national sales! Everyone knew of my reputation from the lowest sales secretary at the branch office to the President of Chevrolet Motor Division and the General Motors President!

The start of a new problem was my salary. Since Motors Holding was retaining the financial paper, they would control my income to allow me only to draw a $75,000 salary and even that made me the highest paid dealer candidate in history. Now think about it. A $75,000 salary is pretty respectful, right? The average family income was just under $20,000, and the minimum wage was $3.80 per hour. Considering that I made seven times more than that the year before made this a significant change in lifestyle!

I had a couple of beach properties both of which I had on a sales agreement that was supposed to settle a couple of weeks after settlement at the dealership and net me a tidy $300,000 profit. That deal quickly fell through, and I had to carry those two mortgages. Winter was upon us and no rental income to pay for the properties. I didn't owe a dime on my personal residence, but I didn't have that sold either; so, I used all the equity in that property as well. Now all of a sudden, I have three mortgages that I have to carry on my small salary.

I couldn't afford to buy a house close to my dealership; so, I had to commute 200 miles every day to and from work. I would leave the house at 6:30 or 7:00 AM and drive to work in rush hour; white knuckled, bumper to bumper traffic six days a week and then do the same thing each night leaving the dealership at 9:00 PM so I could be home by 11:00 PM. I never saw my family. My wife and kids had no life except for waiting for me to show up totally exhausted every night! No more driving home for dinner every night, no more going to my kids sporting events, or more boating, or beach weekends. Saturday was the only saving grace I would allow myself to go in a little later leaving the house about 8:00 AM or so and only working until 5:00 PM. By the time Sunday rolled around, I was numb. I remember listening to a Rich Mullins song, time after time on my trips to and from work. Rich was a favorite Contemporary Christian Singer-Songwriter. The song was entitled "Ready for the Storm," and just a few of the lines went like this: "The waves crash in, the tide rolls out," and the song closed with "Oh, I am ready for the storm. Yes, Sir ready, I am ready for the storm!" And I was tossed around beyond my wildest dreams.

The dealership had bug problems, environmental issues, drug problems, cars being stolen one right after another, money walked in the front and quickly out the back door and if that wasn't enough we were not profitable. I think the only person not stealing from the company was my controller and me. Not being able to hire or keep good employees was only the beginning of my problems.

In the next year and a half, I lost over 35 cars to grand theft at the dealership. We couldn't figure it out at first. The vehicles went missing, and we could never figure out how the thieves were getting them out of a blocked and locked fenced-in storage lot. At least until my service manager, and I stayed there several nights and observed the lot and to discover one of our employees from the recon-shop selling keys to a group of car thieves.

The crooks would show up in the middle of the night, cut the link that held the fence to the post, and drive the cars out right underneath the fence. The fence was so old and rusted that it would stretch and then fly back into place for no one to notice how the cars were escaping the storage lots. It was genius!

My attorney was as sharp as they come; he tried to protect me every way he could. After all, that is their job, isn't it? When we signed the buy-sell agreement with the former owner, my attorney had a portion of the previous owner's proceeds retained and escrowed in the amount of $50,000 to take care of any environmental issues with the property. The bad news is we spent three times that amount resolving all the problems left behind by the former owner. This car dealership was precisely like the Tom Hanks movie, *The Money Pit*.

Each Monday morning would produce a new set of circumstances and problems when I would show up for work at the dealership. One weekend, only to be discovered during my Monday morning arrival, there were 29 cars vandalized. The locals had jumped from car roof to roof; trunk to the roof, then roof to the hood and slid down the windshields onto the hoods. Every brand-new car in that storage lot had extensive damage. It cost me $35,000 out of pocket to cover the insurance deductibles, and then, of course, I had to sell them at deeply discounted prices because I had to disclose that they were damaged goods.

I never knew each day what I would discover until I arrived at the dealership; salespeople were not showing up due to a drug overdose, policemen arresting employees for spousal abuse. One Monday, I found a concrete block that was thrown through the showroom window, onto the hood of a brand-new Corvette Convertible in the corner of the showroom. Every day was quite an adventure, and different from the one before. The best one was the employee who was selling the car keys, who took us to court for Racial Discrimination and Prejudices and wanted remuneration for his lost wages and personal hardships. I am happy to say he lost the court battle months later!

The first day of business we scheduled a full-page ad in the local newspaper. We had 118 ups (that's people) come through the door with the advertisement in their hands with the intentions to buy an automobile from us. We sold 28 cars that day but were able to deliver only two cars due to bad credit and bankruptcies on the other 26 sales. This was nothing like I had ever experienced before. The vast majority of customers that we attracted were deadbeats, and so were our salespeople. This Chevrolet dealership was known as the last place in town you wanted to sell cars or buy a car. I came from a beautiful rural area where people paid their bills on time, and their word meant something. If we sold 28 cars in a day, we would deliver 26 or 27 of them.

We moved the sales needle: the dealership was selling about 35 cars a month when we took over and our best month was 235 cars. But between all the problems, it eventually overwhelmed me and sank me into a deep depression. What was once a bright shining star of potential had been blown out like a flaming meteor. I had a chance to sell the dealership to my neighboring dealer who owned quite a few profitable dealerships in the market and had an excellent reputation for sales and service. This would have been a slam dunk buy/sell deal, with me not losing a dime of my investment. But, Chevrolet didn't want him as their dealer of choice. They wanted a candidate or owner with a different profile for this location, so Chevrolet chose their own guy! It took Chevrolet almost a year to get their guy in there and approved, and when I left the closing table that day, I left with my tail tucked between my legs, depressed, and a measly check for $5001. Remember, I put a down payment of $675,000 and left with a check of $5001.

I never forgot that ride home that day. It was the longest, loneliest, saddest ride I ever had in my life. I burned through my retirement, my stocks, bonds, properties, and every liquid asset I could dispose of. So, did I allow that voice to talk me into failure, or was it my destiny? Did God put me in there to fail?

PATIENCE— ## WHAT I MEANT TO SAY WAS…

Sometimes when a door closes, you have to know when to quit tugging on that handle and quit looking for another way to get in that door. There's an old saying, "When God closes a door, there's probably an open window." To this day, I'm not sure why I failed so miserably. I look back and think, "I was living a wholesome life with truth in it for a change, and my best intentions were to make a difference in people's lives in the community." I think, what I should have said to myself at the time was, "Be more patient!" Patience is something that all of us need to learn. And patience is something that has never come easy for me. I want it, I want it now, and will do almost anything to get it now. And this pertained to most anything in my life from business to my personal life.

When I had gone to work at the Chevy store that I left before my own dealership, the last thing that dealer told me was, "If we do well, I promise, I will give you a buy-in!" A year had come and gone by now, and the owner was making millions in net profit, and he wasn't about to sell at this point. It would have served my situation better by working the three or so years. After all, I was probably the highest paid car dealership general manager in the country. No one had the benefits, the flexibility, and the income that I had, but that wasn't enough for me. I wanted my own shingle and my name on my car dealership! If I would have pursued my advertising agency full time at that current moment, I could have probably retained that account. It was a big account at the time, and I had grown my advertising business with the two employees I had at the time. My reputation was flawless in the industry; doors were opening left and right, but I was impatient!

When I left my old dealership, sales quickly receded to their former sales numbers, almost overnight. The last full month I was there we delivered well over 500 cars that month. The first month I was gone, the dealership delivered 410 units, then to 280 units the very next month and sales continued spiraling downward, accompanied by a mass exodus of critical sales managers and great salespeople.

The owner felt the bleeding coming on quickly, and he was smart enough to sell to a reliable dealer group, but had I been patient, it very well could have been my dealership! That would have been nice, no two-hour commute, no relocating, and I could have rounded up the same staff, without burning through nearly three-quarters of a million dollars!

What if I had not made any changes to the dealership I bought? I say change nothing, with the exception that I take over the front of the house sales department and build it as I did for so many others.

I had to learn patience, but I wanted to be the most significant overnight!

How Can This Help You?

It was the first time in my life where I could sit back and realize that I should have been more patient. When it's said that patience is a virtue, they're not kidding. It's not something that is learned quickly or easily! So, practice it whenever you can and be patient and wait on the Lord!

"Rejoice in hope, be patient in tribulation, be constant in prayer." (Romans 12:12 ESV)

"But if we hope for what we do not see, we wait for it with patience." (Romans 8:25 ESV)

"And let us not grow weary of doing good, for in due season we will reap, if we do not give up." (Galatians 6:9 ESV)

"Be still before the Lord and wait patiently for him; fret not over the one who prospers in his way, over the man who carries out evil devices! Refrain from anger and forsake wrath! Fret not yourself; it tends only to evil. For the evildoers shall be cut off, but those who wait for the Lord shall inherit the land." (Psalm 37:7–9 ESV)

"For I know the plans I have for you, declares the Lord, plans for welfare and not for evil, to give you a future and a hope." (Jeremiah 29:11 ESV)

"Do not be anxious about anything, but in everything by prayer and supplication with thanksgiving let your requests be made known to God." (Philippians 4:6 ESV)

Literally weeks before settling on the sale of the car dealership, I finally sold my beach houses and my personal residence. Now the only problem was where my family will live. I have no money; fortunately, God allowed my credit to remain intact, but still, I have no money. In fact, I had over $50,000 in debt after paying all the creditors from the car dealership and after refinancing my properties. What a life-changing experience! An experience I wouldn't pay a nickel for, but wouldn't give it up for a million dollars.

Last, but not least, don't allow your past success to get in the way of the real problems that exist in a project. Remember, you are not superman, and each one of us has limited skills no matter how good we think we are. It's almost impossible for you to create chicken salad from chicken crap! Quit trying to fix something that doesn't want or need to be fixed, and this wouldn't be the last time in my life I attempt this feat!

Chapter 16

ONE DOOR CLOSES, ANOTHER DOOR OPENS

I'm in Florida; I had just gotten back from a beautiful, long, early-morning run on the beach to the hotel we were staying at in Long Boat Key. I open the door to my room and see the telephone light blinking on the desk. "Who called while I was out?" I wondered. Checking the voicemail and it's a message, I find that it's from the auto dealer I went to work for after I sold my dealership. "Bill, I won't need your services any longer here at our dealership. We are going to take a different route than your leadership role. Please feel free to keep your wife's demonstrator as well as your demonstrator if you need it. We are mailing your last paycheck to you with your bonus for the month."

My mind was overflowing with thoughts. "What am I going to do now?" I have no ready cash available, and I had just bought a new home using a credit card for the down payment! "How am I going to pay the loans back?" I am not going back into the car business or ever work for anyone again in my life under any circumstances. The thoughts continue circling my mind. My new home needs landscaping, there are three inches of water in the basement, and no deck or steps on the back of the house. What am I going to do? I have no money, my savings are gone, and my credit cards are at their limit. I have two children and a stay at home wife that depends on me for support, income, and stability. "What am I going to do now?"

I am persuaded by friends and my family to start my advertising agency as my new full-time career. I have no choice, but to try to dry my wet basement and finish a rear entrance to get possible clients and future employees into my downstairs home-based office.

When I get home from Florida, I immediately call my carpenter friend to help me finish a deck and a set of steps from the driveway around the back of our new house to the entrance of what will be my office at the rear of the house. After a couple of weeks, we managed to get the basement dried out, a deck and entrance finished, and we're ready to do business.

What equipment I previously owned from my in-house advertising agency was in storage in town, and now that equipment had made its way to our new home to be set up for business. I own enough stuff to start a full-blown ad agency, but I must tell you, I have no clue how half of the machinery works. If that's not enough, I am now about to start an ad agency from the ground up without having money, without having employees, or money to pay employees!

Every day, I dress in my suit and tie, armed, and ready to do business that day and start my regimen of prospecting for a company that is desperately needed. I had a "good stick," or as some call it, a sales pitch for selling my services. I had a lot of success in the car business, I had taken more dealerships from the toilet and made them profitable than I cared to remember, and now I was putting those ideas into practice in the form of marketing plans and advertising for future full-time clients! My office was off limits to the children from 8:00 in the morning until 5:00 PM. Everyone in the house knew this was our family business; no dogs, no cats, and no kids were allowed, and no interruptions during business hours, period!

I was fortunate to get a couple of freelance artists to do work for me at the onset; and after a few hours of training, I was capable of at least designing a header or two for an ad on the computer. The paste-up artist would then put the layouts together with my instruction, and then we would shoot a stat of them with the stat camera. I accomplished most of this by the seat of my pants. I never really had or set foot in a real ad agency. I had a good idea from experience of how it should run or work, so it didn't take long to get started with the basics of "Auto Advertising 101."

After a month or two, I had a couple of clients and was shipping ads, cutting radio, and TV commercials to the point where I could hire a full-time designer who had a little more computer savvy than I had. Oh, what a disaster this had become, my first freelance artist lost his driver's license and had to ride his bicycle to my office. That would have been okay, but he lived 30 miles away, and he wasn't precisely Lance Armstrong. Also, the fall season was rapidly approaching, and along with fall came shorter daylight hours, so by 5:00 or 6:00 PM it was dark.

The time had come for my first full-time employee, but with that came buying additional computer equipment for which I had no money. It got so tight financially; my mother showed up one day in her little Volkswagen Super Beetle with a car full of groceries. There were bags full of hamburger, chicken, pork chops, fruit and vegetables, lots of toilet paper, and plenty of paper towels, about 20 bags in all. What a blessing this was. I never thought that my retired mother would be buying her son groceries, who made half a million dollars a year just a couple of years ago.

I had a designer that worked for me at my in-house agency at the car dealership. I thought she would be a great prospect as an employee, so I called her. She was working at the local newspaper in her town. She had a liking for me, my wife, and kids. So, she decided she would make a trip to visit us and I talked her into coming to work at our new advertising agency. We had an extra bedroom in the house with a private bathroom, so she would drive about 100 miles on Monday morning, work and stay the week, and then head home Friday night after we met the deadlines.

This arrangement worked out nicely for a few months, and soon I was able to hire another employee and relieve her of her duties. We had good growth, and it took a couple of years, but we grew to several million dollars in annual revenue and eventually about five or six full-time employees before I had to hire a person to do the accounting and billing.

Every year produced substantial business increases and profits to the point where I hired a copywriter, media buyer, and my first full-time salesperson. We were finally completely out of room at the house with eight full-time employees. I was able to put enough cash together, which allowed us to buy an old firehouse building at public sale, along with a remodeling loan to suit our growing business needs!

BEYOND MY WILDEST DREAMS— WHAT I MEANT TO SAY WAS...

Talk about a spineless guy who didn't even have the courtesy to fire me face-to-face. As an employer, you must have guts. If you don't dare to do the hard things in business, then don't ever become an employer! Being a boss isn't for weenies! So, I thanked him for forcing me to change my course of life and get me away from working for someone else once again!

For me, this was one of the most significant opportunities of my life. I didn't know it at the time, but it turned out to be an opportunity beyond my wildest dreams! After I sold the Chevy store, I thought that I would never have the earning potential that I had in the car business. That thought could not have been further from the truth. Trust God and allow Him to put you where He wants you.

HOW CAN THIS HELP YOU?

This situation gave me more free time to go to my children's softball games, track meets, basketball games, and more. It allowed me the freedom to build my business and work for myself on my terms. Sometimes, we are forced to look at other scenarios in life that we never even considered, and this scenario was one of those situations.

If there's a will, there can be a way—if you're determined to change the course of your current life. Many people who become self-employed are forced into it just like I was. They don't do it by design, there comes a day when their well-paying job comes to an abrupt halt, and they find themselves unemployed, and then the moment of truth strikes!

Estimates vary, but generally, more than 600,000 businesses are started each year in the United States. For every American who starts a business, there are likely millions more who begin each year saying "Okay, this is the year I am going to start a business," and then they don't.

Everyone has his or her roadblock, something that prevents them from taking that crucial first step. Many people are afraid to start; they may fear the unknown or failure, or even success. Others find beginning something overwhelming in the mistaken belief they must start from scratch. They think they have to come up with something that no one has ever done before—a new invention, or unique service. In other words, they believe they have to reinvent the wheel, but you don't have to! Start with what you know and love and change or improve it as you go!

But the big question usually is, "Do I go to work for someone else or try to make it on my own?" And the person with guts will say, "I'm not doing this any longer, I can do it myself. I've done for other people what I can do for myself!"

And one final thought! Only 10 percent of individuals have a desire to be self-employed, and of the 10 percent that think about it, only 10 percent of those people will do something about it. Fifty percent of small businesses fail within the first year, and ten years down the road just 7 percent of those businesses will remain. So, when you take that leap to become self-employed, do your math, repeatedly, and be ready for the thrill of a lifetime!

Chapter 17

THE MESSAGE

In and out of brain fog—weary from a long day's work the night before—I find myself tuning into the pastor's message. I hear this voice, instructing me to get involved to help a local youth ministry in my community. As I hear, "get involved with them!"—my answer back, to what I truly believe was the Holy Spirit speaking to my heart about being more involved was this! I thought to myself, "How am I going to get involved in this kids' ministry? I just started my advertising agency. I don't have the kind of money necessary to ignore my growing business!" And the words came quickly again in response to the voice in my head. "Don't worry, get involved, and sink your heart and soul into this ministry!" And again, my answer was, "How can I do this?" "Don't worry, just do it, and your business will grow beyond your wildest dreams."

I took God's advice and lived every minute for Him, and my business did grow beyond my wildest dreams! Over the next few years, you could see God growing this ministry from one full-time and one part-time employee with about an $85,000 annual budget to about seven or eight full-time employees and an annual budget of well over $500,000. The original mortgage was paid off, their single largest fundraiser—a benefit auction—went from $10,000 a year to more than $200,000 in a three-day event.

My advertising agency helped in virtually every category of the auction, collecting over 500 autographed items for their annual sale. This came about from all the sports contacts that I had made through major sports teams and my growing business. Also, several hundred pieces of art, automobiles, trips, tickets, woven baskets, and 1000s of used items would be collected every year for this event. Many of our advertising agency full-time employees had a crucial role in growing the annual auction 2000 percent over the next 12 years.

God was faithful to His words that He spoke quietly to me that day in the pew at my church. My agency went from several hundred thousand dollars in revenue to over 20 million dollars, and from one full-time employee to a new 2.9-million-dollar facility with 35 full-time employees.

Diversification was happening in my life in more ways than one—a clothing store was purchased, parking lots were acquired, rental properties, and more. Amid all this, I was soon recognized as a downtown developer with a new downtown vision. I started a 12-million-dollar impact project with the revitalization of a couple of city blocks, including the original Farmers Market, an upscale restaurant, and a café. This project also included the demolition of one of the biggest downtown eyesores, making way for downtown parking of another 90 vehicles at the busiest intersection in the county.

Our clothing store was growing at a torrid pace to 1.5 million dollars in sales and now included women's clothing as well, and it was recognized as the best apparel store in the valley. The restaurant would do $2.2 million in sales being known as the best new restaurant in six or seven counties, and the following three years as the best restaurant. There was one magazine cover story right after another. One featured me as, "The Man About Town" with a six or seven-page feature story! When that magazine article hit the newsstands, I remembered thinking to myself, "If they only knew!"

I was living in duality with a secret life of lies! Multiple marital affairs, a separation was leading to an eventual divorce. All the while, the youth ministry was watching from the wings as I was destroying my life and getting ready to go down in flames. The director of the ministry came to my palatial office one day and asked me to resign from the ministry because of my un-Christian like extra-curricular behaviors. Not long after that meeting, they told me they would no longer accept my monetary gifts to the ministry!

Now, my divorce was final to the tune of—well let's just say—a lot of money. The agency which I was fighting for control of in my divorce settlement went from $20 plus million in sales to less than half that to $9.6 million in one year. The following year it went all the way down to $2.8 million in sales. I gave up my 401k retirement account to keep my head above water for a brief period, and I sold my very expensive custom-built hotrod to pay back a loan from a friend. My agency was no longer a cash cow, but now a dead dog, bleeding real losses every month for the first time ever. The restaurant sales had dropped more than 50 percent, as I searched for a new owner and the clothing sale was in the middle of a "going out of business sale."

When I sold my car dealership many years before, I remember thinking I'll never have the earning potential that I had in the car business. That thought could not have been further from the truth. It took 20 years to build this incredible lifestyle that all I had to do was do what God asked me to do for it to continue for life. But the minute I turned and ignored God's plan for me, and once I started to go my own direction, it only took a few short years before I was living in a deep, dark hole of depression—bankrupt personally and professionally!

USE HIS PLAN BOOK— WHAT I MEANT TO SAY WAS...

If a man or woman is called of God, it doesn't matter how difficult the circumstances may be. God orchestrates every force at work for His purpose in the end. Remember, "He's God, and we are not!" If you agree with God's purpose, He will bring not only your conscious level but also all the deeper levels of your life—which you cannot reach—into perfect harmony! God did this for me in so many ways, but I was easily swayed into believing I can do anything. We are taught to believe you can do anything if God is laying those plans for you, but when you no longer allow yourself to use His plan book, things will change. Believe me, I know from experience!

I was always cautious with my donations—as I've mentioned before—to never allow the right hand to know what the left hand is doing, but I think this verse is a critical verse in life for me:

> *"Beware of practicing your righteousness before other people to be seen by them, for then you will have no reward from your Father who is in heaven. When you give to the needy, sound no trumpet before you as the hypocrites do in the synagogues and in the streets, that they may be praised by others. Truly, I say to you, they have received their reward. But when you give to the needy, do not let your left hand know what your right hand is doing, so that your giving may be in secret. And your Father who sees in secret will reward you."* (Matthew 6: 1–4)

A lot of individuals got hurt financially through my recklessness with my downtown project. It wasn't just the expensive divorce and family relationships that can barely be repaired; the banks and the City lost millions from unpaid loans, and contractors, suppliers, and jobbers lost money as well. Some outstanding former employees ended up being unemployed and without jobs for a long time. But I don't think any of the employees got any more hurt than I did, with what I did to break God's heart!

HOW CAN THIS HELP YOU?

This experience has been the most humbling and grounding thing that has ever happened to me. It seems I always measured my self-worth by my accumulation of wealth, financial items, such as expensive houses, cars, motorcycles, antiques, and by my donations. When you are stripped of everything financially, you quickly learn who your friends are as well. The bandwagon jumpers, the people waiting to drink or eat on your dime, and ex-employees disappear like a thief in the night when things no longer benefit them. There is one, however, who sticks closer than a brother. Remember, no matter how you fail in this life, Jesus will never leave you or forsake you. Knowing this is crucial to a happy, prosperous future.

> *"Keep your lives free from the love of money and be content with what you have, because God has said, 'Never will I leave you; never will I forsake you.'"* (Hebrews 13:5)

I think this time in my life helped me realize that it's not what you have or what you give that makes you happy, but the joy of a risen Savior who has already overcome this life.

> *"I have told you these things, so that in me you may have peace. In this world you will have trouble. But take heart! I have overcome the world."* (John 16:33)

It also made me realize that a man isn't measured by what he has, or by what he has accumulated in life, but the relationships that he has with his children, his wife, and his friends who remain after the dust has settled. But even these can fail at times—most important is your connection and relationship with God your Father—knowing that He loves you and will always be with you—He will never fail you.

> *"One who has unreliable friends soon comes to ruin, but there is a friend who sticks closer than a brother."* (Proverbs 18:24)

Occasionally, when you least expect it, you'll get that call, card, or email of encouragement. Most other so-called friends and bandwagon jumpers probably will never be heard from again, and that's okay, you won't miss them either! Most awesomely, you can always hear from the One who created you and gave you all your giftings by opening His book and spending time with Him. He will ever meet you wherever you're at—no pit is too deep, no mountain too high, that he can't instantly meet you wherever you are.

Chapter 18

"I DO" TURNED OUT TO BE "I DON'T!"

My alarm sounded and woke me up promptly at 6:00 AM. I jumped out of bed, it was a typically cold and snowy February morning. Yes, that's right, my very own version of the movie, *Groundhog Day*. I had a huge presentation and speech to give that morning at the State of the City Annual Breakfast. It was the largest attended breakfast meeting of the year for the city. I was the guest speaker and scheduled to present my revitalization plan for the new downtown!

My wife was already out of bed for some reason, but I didn't pay too much attention to it at the time. Whenever I had a speaking engagement, or an important business meeting scheduled, I would always prearrange my clothing the night before; my suit hanging from my armoire, draped in front would be my freshly starched shirt with the perfect accenting neck-tie, cuff-links, silk pocket square, socks, shoes, and of course, my coordinating eyewear. All the accessories that matched perfectly symbolizing:

"He's well put together, just like everything he does." After all, "A good first impression is a lasting impression!"

When I finished taking my shower and came out of the bathroom, I rounded the corner, towel wrapped around me. I looked at my armoire, and to my amazement, my clothing was gone! The clothing that I had meticulously laid out the night before—which had been hanging there just before I jumped into the shower—was now missing. Without overthinking, I headed to my walk-in closet and to my further amazement my closet was completely barren, cleaned out! Emptier than ole Mother Hubbard's cupboard! When I turned around to walk out of the closet, I looked out of my closet window and glanced in the front yard, and to my now blown away amazement, all my clothing was thrown outside onto the freshly fallen February snow below. Over 100 silk neckties, 50 boxes of shoes, suits, sport-coats, shirts, and belts ended up in the snow. Everything was tossed out of my closet into the snowy February weather. It was like one of those email photos that floated around the country several hundred times. I'm sure you've seen it; the guy's boat is parked in front of his house with each of his last possessions just piled into the boat, and spray painted on the side it reads, "Cheating Bastard." Well, this was one of those Kodak moments for the neighborhood.

Here I am, nothing but a towel wrapped around me and nothing to wear! I quickly pulled a pair of jeans and a tee-shirt out of the dirty clothes hamper, grabbed some previously worn socks and headed downstairs. I opened the hall closet with the hopes of finding a coat and boots, something to help me sort through my discovery in the snow-covered front yard; but nothing in the closet either! My coat closet was emptied out as well. I headed out through the garage to my SUV, and all my coats, boots and scarves were scattered on the floor in a heap in the garage, and still no wife to be found.

I ran upstairs, and my wife was now in the midst of emptying my armoire. She had the bedroom window wide open and proceeded to empty my sock and underwear drawers. My sweaters were in the process of being hurled out the window, into the new snow in the front yard to accompany the rest of my wardrobe. Most guys would have become angry with what was happening to their belongings. But, I figured, let her blow off her steam, and then we'll talk. I tried to stop her for just a second, and all I kept thinking about was her trying to accuse me of hurting her, so I immediately allowed her to finish the task of helping me move out once and for all.

Through the pile of rubble, I located a pair of boots and grabbed a coat off the garage floor, jumped into my SUV, and backed my vehicle into the middle of the front yard, and proceeded to load all my clothing into my vehicle carefully. I carefully picked up one item after another, shaking all the snow off my things as I packed them laboriously into my car.

As I was loading my things, a State Police car pulled into the driveway. The officers got out of their cruiser and walked over to me. I immediately asked them, "What's the problem, officers?" And their reply was "We had a call about a domestic disturbance!" And my response was "That's funny, I never called you guys!" And his response was "No, it was a lady that called." He asked for identification which I didn't have. Who knows where my wallet was at this point. It was probably scattered in the snow somewhere. I reached out to shake the officer's hand and told him what my name was, and his response, "Oh, you're the downtown developer that's doing all the revitalization." "Yes, that would be me." And then he proceeded to tell me that my wife made a domestic call to the police barracks indicating she might need assistance with some possible domestic violence. I went into the house and asked her to come outside and tell me what the heck was going on. First, she throws all my clothing out the window in the snow, and then calls the State Police on me! She came outside and said, "Well, I thought you would be angry at me for me throwing all your clothing out into the snow." And my reply was "In 28 years have I ever lifted a hand to you in anger? Have I ever yelled at you in a fit of rage?" And her answer was "No, but I thought you would be really angry with me this time!" The State Policeman said, "This doesn't appear to be a domestic violence situation, but it looks like you two need to work some issues out." And with that, the State Police left.

I continued to load my vehicle, drove in town, and unloaded at my office and then headed to the dry cleaners with the items that were too wrinkled, snowy or soiled to survive a trip to a different closet.

ALLOWING GOD TO FIGHT YOUR BATTLE— WHAT I MEANT TO SAY WAS...

I admit that I was not just the majority of the problem, I was the entire problem! When things had upset me in the past, I should have gone toe to toe with her and settled them. But I steadily looked elsewhere for happiness, and ultimately it turned to affairs, and for that, I am genuinely sorry.

"In your anger do not sin': Do not let the sun go down while you are still angry." (Ephesians 4:26)

Allow God to fight your battle, we are not equipped to fight a battle when Satan is involved! God hates divorce. Satan will figure out a way to make it alright no matter what you are doing. In hindsight, I know I should have made our marriage work, but after going back and forth time after time, I never could! I know I did wrong things to her, and it haunts me every day how I broke up one of God's plans.

I discovered nearly 50 Bible verses on divorce, 50 verses on adultery, and well over 50 verses on forgiveness. I think that at the time I was manipulating the system, in regard to God's word, and my chance to get out of a relationship that I was unhappy in for years. But you know what? It may be many years later, but you'll be reminded of what you have broken apart, that God put together. You might not think so at the time, because all you want is out, but the kids are affected, and even the grandchildren pay a part in the future pain.

Finally, after many years I have learned to fear the Lord. These verses make me feel a little less convicted, and that my business and personal life were not being suffocated because of my past sins. Read Psalm 103:

> *"The Lord is compassionate and gracious, slow to anger, abounding in love. He will not always accuse, nor will He harbor His anger forever; he does not treat us as our sins deserve or repay us according to our iniquities. For as high as the heavens are above the earth, so great is His love for those who fear him; as far as the east is from the west, so far has He removed our transgressions from us.*
>
> *As a father has compassion on his children, so the Lord has compassion on those who fear him; for He knows how we are formed, he remembers that we are dust. The life of mortals is like grass, they flourish like a flower of the field; the wind blows over it, and it is gone, and its place remembers it no more. But from everlasting to everlasting the Lord's love is with those who fear Him, and his righteousness with their*

children's children—with those who keep his covenant and remember to obey his precepts." (Psalms 103:8–18)

Here is another helpful piece of good news, it comes from Luke 11:

"So, I say to you: Ask, and it will be given to you; seek and you will find; knock and the door will be opened to you. For everyone who asks receives; the one who seeks finds; and to the one who knocks, the door will be opened.

Which of you fathers, if your son asks for a fish, will give him a snake instead? Or if he asks for an egg, will give him a scorpion? If you then, though you are evil, know how to give good gifts to your children, how much more will your Father in heaven give the Holy Spirit to those who ask Him!" (Luke 11:9–13)

It says, "Ask, it will be given to you!" So, if I want forgiveness, all I must do is ask, and then believe it, and it is done. Not do this, do that, stand on your head and spit nickels... no, it's done, just ask!

How Can This Help You?

There was a beautiful message I heard at the church I then attended. It was speaking about: "just Jesus," it was a hard-hitting message that talked about forgiveness and moving on!

Moving on is a hard thing to do, whether it's concerning a death, a substantial financial loss, debilitating illness, or a painful end of a longtime relationship. Holding onto resentment and the pain of the past will only keep you back in your recovery of moving on. President Lyndon B. Johnson said this:

"Yesterday is not ours to recover, but tomorrow is ours to win or lose!"

I am a bottom line kind of guy. Unless you forgive yourself and let go, you can't move on, and when Jesus talks about forgiveness, He's not only speaking about us forgiving others. He is referring to us forgiving ourselves as well!

Chapter 19

FORGIVE ME, GOD, FOR WHAT I'M ABOUT TO DO!

I am driving west on the interstate highway, and I have a feeling that my personal life is out of control. My very eyes are revealing the real me. My businesses were doing fine, my building projects were slowly showing signs of vitality, and the monies I had been promised from the state budget system were slowly starting to trickle in. But my personal life is in the tank, deep in the tank.

By this point, I have already been asked by the director of the ministry I was involved in to step down and to resign permanently from the ministry. That request proved to be a blow to my ego that would hurt for a long time. My marital separation was also going strong with money going to my estranged wife and attorneys as fast as I could earn it. And if that wasn't enough, my daughters disapproved of the lifestyle I was leading. I was no longer being a man of honor, a man of integrity, or any of the things that I wanted to be known for. But even with all that pressure tugging at my heart, I still wanted to have a relationship with a woman I had met across the river. This was a relationship that I knew was unhealthy… but I was about to continue it because it felt so good now!

I was very successful and an easy target for Satan. He and his demonic little underlings were on to me and my lustful desires and would do anything to have me struggle and to let me give in to my selfish desires and temptations, repeatedly.

It's a hot summer day, and I'm able to escape work for some extra-curricular activity. I was headed westbound with such conviction that I prayed to God: "Forgive me for what I am about to do!" How sick am I personally and so lost spiritually to pray such a prayer? Praying a prayer that God would allow me to sin and come out the other side unscathed, unburned, and unharmed couldn't have been further from the truth in God's eyes!

I made the trip and continued to make the trip, but every brick in my wall would be pulled out one at a time. My financial wall would be destroyed in no time—after taking nearly 20 years to build a life of comfort and integrity! I wonder why God didn't have me grab the steering wheel and pull it right into a bridge abutment or the river.

THE COST OF SIN— WHAT I MEANT TO SAY WAS…

It had to be just like God looking at Lot's wife in Sodom and Gomorrah as God looked down on me at that moment. Oh, how I wish he would have turned me into a pillar of salt!

A pastor of mine, one time said this many years ago, and I even wrote the note down in my Bible:

"Sin will take you farther than you want to stray! Sin will keep you longer than you want to stay! Sin will cost you more than you want to pay!"

I've never forgotten those harsh, yet truer words!

How Can This Help You?

I think for the first time in my life, I didn't want to keep cheating on God! I was so convicted by my past actions I knew I had to give up. I think very few people really understand conviction—conviction of sin, by sin, from sin! This is what I read from Oswald Chambers:

"But conviction of sin by the Holy Spirit blots out every relationship on earth and makes us aware of only one!"

Also, in Psalms:

"Against you, you only, have I sinned and done what is evil in your sight; so that you are right in your verdict and justified when you judge." (Psalms 51:4)

I know that God forgives us of our sins, but I know it cost the breaking of His heart with grief in the death of Christ to enable Him to do so!

So, while we cheapen ourselves, we are in confining quarters. We limit ourselves when we are enclosed in self, but we come up from the grace and emerge from the prison and enter the immensity of God and the liberty of his children and we become indeed set free by our Father.

"If anyone thinks they are something when they are not, they deceive themselves." (Galatians 6:3)

I've enjoyed the writing of Beth Moore and her book, *Get out of that Pit.* I found her writing very interesting, considering that I was living in the pit at that time; a pit with my relationships, business, and so on. Beth referred to this in her book. There are three kinds of pits: one you get "thrown" into, which could be from child molestation, rape, or an alcoholic parent or something like that, that you really have little control of. The second one you "slip" into from circumstance like a drug addiction, an affair that you really didn't want to happen, and finally the third one you "jump" into. This one is the most stupid one, and I've done it myself many times. When you take the plunge into a pit that you're aware of, and you know that what you're about to do is wrong, probably even foolish—you have no one to blame but yourself. Whatever the reason, the escalating desire to do it exceeds the good sense not to do it, which is unlike the second one where you slip into it before you really know what's happening!

There is another great read that helped me through my dark times as well, and that would be a book titled, *There's a Hole in the Sidewalk,* by Portia Nelson, and it starts like this:

"I walk down the street.
There is a deep hole in the sidewalk.
I fall in.
I am lost... I am helpless.
It isn't my fault.
It takes forever to find a way out."

After several attempts to walk down the same street, she realizes they must change; open their eyes and see things as they really are, so they step down another road. It's worth the read. You can read this or any of her other writings online or pick up her books in any bookstore.

Chapter 20

THE CEREMONY

It's a gorgeous day downtown; the weather is perfect with the sun shining brightly above. There is no humidity, and it's a perfect 73 degrees. I am not necessarily referring only to the weather; this is a day unlike many of the residents have seen around here for a long time. This is a day that reminds me of the downtown "Prosperity Days" of old. People were hustling and bustling on the sidewalks, cars stopping to allow foot traffic to cross the busy streets, and I am at the epicenter of it all! I am about to be introduced to hundreds of joyous locals for the Farmers Market ribbon cutting ceremony!

It's a beautiful life when you have a great friend sing his rendition of the famous Frank Sinatra song about you, and you know, "The Best is Yet to Come"! The streets are barricaded off for a city block. City, county, and state government offices are at a stand-still today because every dignitary is at the Market House ribbon cutting ceremony. It seems like it took the Master of Ceremonies the better part of an hour to introduce everyone, including representation from the United States

Congress. Our State Senator, various secretaries of agriculture, and others were there, just waiting for their chance to congratulate me and, of course, take their due credit as well! The Governor had his oversized cardboard check for presentation as well. It was the largest joint government-private sector revitalization project in the State's history. The Governor had 38 projects going on statewide like this one, but ours was given an award for the best in the state and the poster child for downtown revitalization!

City officials, investors, and other market house owners throughout the state were continually visiting our facility, all wanting to duplicate the charm and success of our Farmers Market. Because of the victory, we were invited to the State Capitol to do a video on our plan. Beyond that, we were asked on several occasions to come to other towns and do consulting for downtown revitalization plans. I know that I have made a difference in our downtown with the renovations to one of the best farmers markets in the country, and I've started changing our center, not only for my generation but for generations to come.

Like most small towns, our little city was not destroyed in one generation. I think it took place in two or possibly several generations. But in time, we will, and we have reversed the process. As I look back when my daughters were children, it was a thrill to take them to work on Saturdays and have the pleasure to see their beautiful innocent smiles as you help people feel happiness from buying something from you. People have invested in our hometown because we have made a difference with the hope that this town hasn't seen for many generations. People approach us on the street and thank us for what we're doing. Oh, how I love to look at the difference we are making, and you just can't find that on a balance sheet. This is one of those parts of life or an event that I so wish I had a mate to share all this. But I have made the decision to go the way of divorce.

We've provided employment and quality of life for people that no one else would have ever given a chance or believed in, the way I did. When I die, I hope people don't cry at my funeral, I hope they never say he was cheap and lived for himself. I hope that I leave this world knowing that I've left this world a better place than I found it.

After all the introductions had taken place, I'm finally introduced by my good friend, and the MC of the event and my opening words are: "Welcome to my dream!"

I'm very choked up, after all, this was an accomplishment where dreams are made and come to reside. Here is little old me—I flunked eighth grade and dropped out of high school in 11th grade—now I stand before hundreds of people on a blocked off, downtown street about to cut the ribbon on a project that I managed to bring to fruition (of course, with the help of many)! "Oh, my, please, pinch me!"

Just like the Master of Ceremony, I also had people to thank for helping me complete this ambitious project. Oh, there were the politicians—state and local, the bankers, the builders and architects, and everyone in between, but the most significant part of all this was to be able to work side-by-side with my daughters. This day must be every man's dream, and I could have never have done it without their help and support!

I spoke about life's lessons that were taught to me by my big brother. As a child, I was very good at taking things apart, but I was awful at putting them back together. He taught me how to pay attention when you take something apart, so you know how to put it back together. Here was not just one building that I put back together, but the better part of a city block!

The very same day, moments after we filled the streets for the ribbon cutting ceremony, we moved upstairs for the grand opening of my restaurant. A restaurant named after my father, and a cigar lounge named after his restaurant.

This joyous moment would turn out to be relatively short-lived. Mounting bills from project overruns, combined with my divorce payments, and the downturn in the economy had put a considerable cramp on every business I owned. In the meantime, I had turned the reins of my cash cow advertising agency to the employees to operate. I was so tired of dealing with the "Silver Spoon Club," which I defined as sons or daughters who were heirs to the businesses of the parents'. Sales had gone up for a while, but net profits kept sinking from the day I gave up leadership. Now, with a fledgling business, sales were dropping faster than the prom queen's skirt at homecoming! This turned out to be one of the biggest business mistakes I had ever made.

Within about three years, the raging waters would have overtaken me and washed everything away in my business life. But it didn't go without leaving behind some deep scars and wounds, great lessons and yet still some good memories.

LOSING EVERY DIME— WHAT I MEANT TO SAY WAS...

"Welcome to my dream," should have been, "Welcome to my nightmare!" I was so blessed to be able to do a project of this magnitude, but to have it all eventually collapse would leave wounds and scars for years to come.

You work so hard to put something like this together and to have it pulled from the grasp of your fingertips is beyond words. How did I put this together in the first place? I am a normal human being with an abnormal amount of drive. But God had to have been a part of this, there is no way that I could have done this on my own. This was better than a 12 million-dollar project. With every dollar falling into place at the right time, why did it fail? Only God knows.

What is the old carpenter's saying, "Measure twice, cut once!" And his helper replied "I don't understand. I cut twice, and it is still too short!" I did the math, the forecasts, and the market research; checked it, double checked it, and triple checked it. All the planets were lined up in the right direction at the right time, and yet, I still failed!

Looking back, after everything came crashing down, I wish I could have said: "I'm so sorry to all my friends that I let down! I am so sorry for my children that I couldn't leave a legacy behind for them and their children. Even though they could have cared less about a legacy, it would have been nice to have a huge income producing nest egg. I am sorry for the bankers, my attorney, builders, and everyone in between that got stuck financially after all this was over!"

Several years later I went to a golf tournament, and an old friend made a comment: "Put your hands in your pockets, here comes the crook!" It was comments like that, which made me never want to set foot in the town—that I had loved so deeply and with passion—ever again. I set out to try to make a difference when no one else was willing to stick their neck out for being afraid of getting their head lopped off. I figured that would never happen, but sure enough, it happened, and I lost every dime. The cry of the wounded warriors is "All gave some, and some gave all!" Some of the downtown people gave some, including vendors, bankers, contractors, and more, and I gave all!

How Can This Help You?

This project once again illustrated to me that I am only human. I am not a god, nor do I have special powers to make chicken salad out of chicken crap!

I was blessed to have an incredible mother, who loved me the best way she knew how. She gave me everything she could until she couldn't give anymore. One of the most precious gifts my mother gave me was the gift of love and the gift to believe that I could accomplish anything. This project made me realize that when your friends abandon you when the going gets tough, my family and close friends were there to love me and accept me no matter what. It reminded me of when I was a youngster, and how my sisters would buy me clothing; take me to parades, taking me swimming, share their fun from dates, drive-in movies, and more! The point of all this is, having a thousand friends isn't a miracle. The miracle is having one friend who will stand by you when thousands are against you... the most important friend you can ever have is Jesus.

Again, one of my favorite verses:

"One who has unreliable friends soon comes to ruin, but there is a friend who sticks closer than a brother." (Proverbs 18:24)

A prayer to pray, for those who have fallen into this same situation:

"God, you have truly used me as a servant! Lord, please don't allow me ever to stop thanking you for all you've

done for me, for all you're doing in my life right this very moment. Even on this day, when I struggle knowing I must start life once again all over, I thank you for Your promise that You will never leave me or forsake me—I can do all things through Christ who strengthens me!"

Chapter 21

IF THEY ONLY KNEW

My motionless body lies still, waiting for instructions from my mind as to what to do next. I am awakened, and my brain hurts from the pain inflicted upon myself from everything that I am going through. What shall I do with this day? I lie back in bed, watching the enormous tropical paddle fan overhead spinning around and around, just like my life! I am out of control, and I cannot change my situation or circumstance. I can no longer handle the stress of relationships, ailing businesses, and a divorce. Oh, how I wish I could escape reality. Oh, how I hope I could run and never look back!

As I lie in bed, I'm reminded today of a position that I thought I would never be in again in my life. I even remember my CFO's warning, just days ago that my failed auto dealership experience could happen all over again if things didn't change. I remember vividly how the financial foundation of my auto dealership was weakened. One brick at a time was pulled out from the base, reducing it more and more as each day passed. I see this same pattern now right here and right now! God is going to humble me again financially and bring me to my knees and make me start over one more time! When will I get this part of my life right?

It is Saturday morning, and I finally make my way to the café around the corner for a Caffè Breve. I head back to my house, and I check the pile of mail left at the elevator to my penthouse floors above. I sort through the mail: bill, bill, bill, and finally a magazine, but not just any magazine. This magazine features an article about my downtown revitalization project! My Penthouse is featured on the cover, and an additional six or seven pages are covering, "The Man About Town!"

I head upstairs in the elevator to the place I call home. The elevator doors open, leaving behind a pair of antique elevator doors from days forgotten. Above them rests a six-foot diameter wooden clock dial that once adorned the city's farmers market from the turn of the century. All this opens to a party room that extends over 50 feet in length, four floors above, overlooking the city's main street. Sixteen feet high, the coffered wood ceilings cover this expansive space accented with several belt driven period fans to keep the air moving throughout the 140-year-old structure.

My penthouse was initially used for entertaining the department store's most exceptional guests, during periodic showings of new fashions or even an occasional private catered party. Now, it was my living quarters and entertainment area.

Exposed original brick walls, modern granite counters that morph into a bar/entertainment area, all fitted out with the best appliances, accompanied by a fully stocked cooler of fine wines and a 500-cigar humidor. Stained glass windows could be seen throughout the place from the original structure dating back to the 1870s, and exotic plants scattered throughout. A big screen TV, along with surround sound in the entertainment area, also an unchanged, huge, floor to ceiling fireplace with intricately stacked brick made it that much easier to forget hard times in this space entitled, "Paradise Found."

I sit down in my manly winged-backed crocodile chair; feet propped on my woven rattan ottoman, lighted with an elaborately sculpted torchière in the seating area across from the fireplace. My hot breve at fingers reach, and the magazine straddling my lap, opened to the article, "The Man About Town!" I begin to read about myself.

As I review the article, I hear the writer's descriptive words puffing me up. Statements like: "foisted his vision," "he could be credited with driving economic vitality," "he created a contemporary scene," and "he designed the place to be and be seen!"

My thoughts go to, "If they only knew the real me! What kind of lie am I living? Who in the world do I think I am?" I am living in a smoke and mirrors filled world that came right out of the House of Cards. I am overextended, alone, and lonely, and no one knows the real me. I am living behind lies and a façade, but still hold the title, "The Man About Town!" What happened to the man of God I was destined to be?

And while I am in the middle of all this, I feel the pains of my past resurfacing: "Repetition Compulsion Behavior Cycle"—doing repeatedly what I know I shouldn't do. I have no control to quit; I know, and I must remember it is about breaking this RCB cycle!

MANAGE YOUR MIND— WHAT I MEANT TO SAY WAS...

My apartment was just an extension of what I intended my life to mimic and be. It was an orderly and serene space, soothing the soul the minute you entered. It was a clean and balanced space in calming colors orchestrated magnificently.

My swagger about town was the façade erected around me, so people couldn't view how much hurt I had deep down inside. The lifestyle that I had developed and was living was never what God intended for me to live. From the very start, I felt as though God was a part of me changing the face of downtown. He just never wanted me to change my look and who I was!

I am good at a lot of things. I am not perfect, mind you, but good at a lot of stuff! Unfortunately, relationships were never one of them! I must learn and resist and overcome my temptation and my sin of adultery, overcome loneliness, and my newest hurt of depression and failure!

These are behaviors I know and understand that I want to change; yet, I can't seem to replace them right now. Love and love addiction; relationships outside one central relationship must be forgotten. God intended for me to have a stable relationship without the lust of the mind and adultery! And most of all, I must run my primary business as I used to, eliminating senior appointed executives that do not have the ability or cannot run a business the way I expect it to be run.

People all over the world have soiled linen or dirt hidden somewhere, and many have a jaded past. But I oversee me, and I haven't done a very good job of leading lately. Who have I become? I am no longer extraordinary. I have become ordinary, wallowing in a land of sin.

It is essential for each one of us to learn how to manage our mind. After many years, I have finally learned that God is far more interested in changing my mind than changing my circumstances.

We all yearn to have God take away all our existing problems. We all know He can—if He chooses to—change our situations, our hurts, pain, sorrow, suffering, sickness, and the sadness in our lives. But the more we know about God's ways, we learn that He wants to work on us first. The transformation won't happen in our lives until we renew our mind, until our thoughts and thought patterns are changed with healthy, wholesome, Godly thoughts!

I must be still and know that God is God, and wait on Him. I know I need healing from my woundedness and from past abandonment in my life! There's always been an action opportunity in my life, a chance for a sexual relationship. I can either be distracted from it or attracted to Jesus to do the right thing, but only I can decide the outcome. That's the only way I'll know what God wants for me.

I must learn to be good at being honest with myself and know my limitations. Each of us has a choice to sin or not, to be faithful or not. I now choose to be committed for the rest of my life. Why? I want to have what people read and know about me, align perfectly with who I am. I can't allow outside feelings to jade what I need—what I must accomplish—but I must focus on what elements are pure, useful, and real.

I have chosen to repair myself and allow myself to be healed by the Ultimate Healer. It's not about others loving me; I must love me! Others cannot meet my needs. Only I can fit my needs. It is not about someone else enhancing me; it is about me improving myself!

How Can This Help You?

I have chosen not to ignore God's plans for me for the balance of my life. My heart is His, and I want to do what He would have me do.

"Above all else, guard your heart, for everything you do flows from it." (Proverbs 4:23)

The reason we were all put on this earth in the first place is to know that God is the Creator of the Universe, who yearns for us to know Him personally. He wants us to pursue Him in everything we do. He wants us to lean on and rely on His experience, His strength, love, justice, holiness, and compassion. So, He says to all who are willing, "Come to me!"

God has incredible powers to which no other being in the world has access. God is omnipotent giving himself control over everything. He is Omnipresent, having the ability to be everywhere at the same time and Omniscient giving only himself full access to all understanding! Unlike us, God knows what will happen tomorrow, next week, next year, the next decade. He says:

"Remember this, keep it in mind, take it to heart, you rebels. Remember the former things, those of long ago; I am God, and there is no other; I am God, and there is none like me. I make known the end from the beginning, from ancient times, what is still to come." (Isaiah 46:8-10)

He knows what has happened in the world yesterday; what will happen today; and has already scripted my ending! More personally, He knew all the things that would happen in my life, good and bad, and how He could assist me—if only I chose to do so! If you do choose Him, He tells us that He can be:

"...our refuge and strength, an ever-present help in trouble." (Isaiah 46:1)

Seek him and you will find Him!

"...seek the LORD your God, you will find him if you seek him with all your heart and with all your soul." (Deuteronomy 4:29)

I have now taken a personal inventory of my strengths as a leader, a manager of a company, a friend, father or husband, and finally even a Christian! Now is the time that I honestly face the facts about my future.

I look at areas such as planning, organization, communication, listening, decision making, and motivation. I go on to list ten strengths that I have as a manager of people, and they are: I am energetic, I motivate and inspire, and I have empathy. I am loyal and will remain humble. I am sincere and responsible, believable and friendly, a doer. I am ambitious and hard-working! I am designed to make things happen, caring and loving, giving and thoughtful, and I bring security to those around me!

I encourage you to do the same. Look at your life and find the things you're good at. Choose one and list your strengths. Focus on these and not your failures!

In one of Zig Ziglar's books, Zig lists these traits of honesty: enthusiasm, one should be intelligent, disciplined, dependable, caring, knowledgeable, humble, hardworking, persistent, loyal, organized, motivated, dedicated, patient, ambitious, energetic, friendly, goal-oriented, personable, responsible, loving, and thoughtful. Not only that, but he is wise, has faith, is a good listener, and has a positive mental attitude. He has a marvelous sense of humor, is an exceptional character and shows tremendous integrity!

The person with all these winning characteristics would make a great leader. This person is you. Seek God with all your heart and ask Him to bless you as you pursue His plan for your life!

Chapter 22

JAILED WITH FAILURE AND DEPRESSION

Shackled with the chains of failure, I am chilled to the deep core of my bones from my damp, cold dungeon that I've made for myself. Fault is with me and controlling me. Failure has consumed me and has taken up permanent residence in my life and mind. I am uncontrollably grasping for something substantial to hold on to, something to try and get my life back on the right track to something positive. My memory is continuously filled with flashbacks of times of joy and happiness, and what my life used to be—times with no financial stress, times of a joyous marriage and relationship. Please give me back those beautiful memories of yesterday, when success was an everyday occurrence, and I could do no financial wrong. Those days now seem long gone, unattainable, and far from my reach as I am linked to failure and depression.

When will God's eyes see favor on me once again? It has been years since my mind has thought positive thoughts, and each day of my life is focused on survival and overcoming my past. The things I had taken for granted are now a distant memory, and all I can speak of is that distant memory of the good life from my past!

Thoughts ramble through my mind, "Maybe, I should try re-opening my advertising agency? How about public speaking or becoming a motivational speaker? Who would want to hear from a failure like me? Maybe, I should sell vacuum cleaners, brushes, or anything to make money? Maybe, I should open a retail store or even a restaurant. Oh, wait. I can't do any of those things, I have no money! I have no assets remaining, and I have terrible credit from my bankruptcy."

The negative onslaught continues, "How will I keep going? How will I persevere? The things of failure and depression have ravaged my mind! Where has my faith gone?"

"By faith Abraham, when called to go to a place he would later receive as his inheritance, obeyed and went, even though he did not know where he was going. By faith he made his home in the Promised Land like a stranger in a foreign country; he lived in tents, as did Isaac and Jacob, who were heirs with him of the same promise. For he was looking forward to the city with foundations, whose architect and builder is God. And by faith, even Sarah, who was past childbearing age, was enabled to bear children because she considered him faithful who had made the promise. And so, from this one man, and he is as good as dead, came descendants as numerous as the stars in the sky and as countless as the sand on the seashore." (Hebrews 11:8-12)

By faith people passed through the Red Sea, the walls at Jericho fell, Jesus brought people back from the dead, and Daniel was saved from the mouths of the lions.

I know and believe in all these things, so where has my faith gone?

My faith has left my mind and is now occupied by failure and depression. Do I have the strength to pull myself up by my bootstraps, one more time? Do I have the faith to allow God to take over my thoughts and consume my mind once again with joy and adoration? Can I remember what God's word says?

> *"Keep your lives free from the love of money and be content with what you have, because God has said, 'Never will I leave you; never will I forsake you.' So, we say with confidence, 'The Lord is my helper; I will not be afraid. What can mere mortals do to me?'"* (Hebrews 13: 5–6)

Right at this moment, I need to learn to manage my emotions because they are too unreliable for what God desires for the balance of my life. I will not allow failure, depression and my feelings to manipulate my thought life. I want to please God again. I want to be a success. I know that God will use me again, and I know that Satan hates when I become healthy and start thinking like I should, for then, I am dangerous to the kingdom of darkness. Satan knows from my past that God will use me in the future!

DREAM BIG DREAMS— WHAT I MEANT TO SAY WAS…

I understand that perseverance means more than merely holding on until the end of my days. I feel stretched as Oswald Chambers puts it in My Utmost for His Highest:

> *"God is aiming at something the saint cannot see, but our Lord continues to stretch and strain and occasionally; the saint says, 'I can't take anymore!' Yet God pays no attention.*

He goes on stretching until His purpose is in sight, and then lets the arrow fly!"

The disaster occurred in my life when I lacked the mental composure that came from establishing the eternal truth that God is Holy love."

I must maintain my relationship with Jesus through the perseverance of faith. I must proclaim as Job did:

"Though He slay me, yet I will hope in Him." (Job 13:15)

I must understand it's the tough times of life that cause us to grow. That's when my faith is stretched the most. That's when God is doing His work in us; it may be uncomfortable, we may not like it, but if we keep a "Yes Attitude,"—as Jeffrey Gitomer talks about—God has promised to use our difficulty for our good! I know He'll use it to my advantage! I know I must be prepared for what God has in store for me. I've said it all along, God has chosen me for this task, and because there was no one else that would come forward to do it or could do it; no one else that would listen to His quiet still voice saying that things will work out. No one else would believe the way things have fallen into place in certain circumstances, time after time, after time. I now know that I am not a failure! We all have bumps in the road, but we will NOT fail, and I know that He is at the helm. I'm stretched... but He's in control, and He knows precisely where the arrow is going! He is using these times to stretch my spiritual muscles, to burn the garbage off me and He is aware of my circumstances. Rick Warren says:

"We are products of our past, but we don't have to be prisoners of it!"

If God is directing my steps, my footing will be firm as it reads about in Psalms:

"The LORD makes firm the steps of the one who delights in him; though he may stumble, he will not fall, for the LORD upholds him with his hand." (Psalm 37:23-24)

What else I find incredible in this is what follows in verse 25:

"I was young and now I am old, yet I have never seen the righteous forsaken or their children begging bread." (Psalm 37:25)

With all that I've been through in my life, the incredible ups, and the gut-wrenching downs, I have never missed a meal. My own children have always been provided for, and I know I am being supplied for right now as I leave the failure and depression of my past behind. Today, I don't worry.

"Look at the birds of the air; they do not sow or reap or store away in barns, and yet your heavenly Father feeds them. Are you not much more valuable than they?" (Matthew 6:26)

I know that God will not allow difficulty to come into my life unless He has a purpose for it. I have also discovered that God likes to outdo Himself constantly. He wants to show His favor in my life in more significant ways than He ever has before. God wants me to be more blessed tomorrow than I was yesterday. He intends for me to have a more substantial impact on the world than I ever have before. What that means is I haven't created my best project yet!

I know that I am a child of the Most High God, and God has breathed His life into me. He's planted seeds of greatness in me. I know I'm full of potential, but I must do my part and start tapping into it. I must make better use of the gifts and talents God has given me. And I know that I have a gift, I have something that no one else has. I have something to offer that no one else can offer. God didn't put me on this earth for mediocrity or by accident. I know that God wants me to accomplish great things for His Honor and Glory. Someone needs what I have to offer!

I am valuable, we all are. We all have treasures hidden inside of each one of us, we need to quit playing that old tune and play a new one. The following are 12 positive thoughts that I say out loud to myself:

1. I am creative.

2. I am anointed and talented.

3. I have a bright future, and my best days are in front of me!

4. I need to think I'm successful because I am!

5. I have the favor of God.

6. People like me are victors, not victims!

7. My potential has been put in me by my Creator, my Manufacturer, by my Almighty God!

8. The events of my past, well, frankly that's just what they are, my past, and we all have one. It is just a matter of what we do with it!

9. I will not reduce the potential of my future in His work and plan.

10. I must be careful not to allow the negative words to play over and over in my mind, they can and have created a stronghold on me, but I will no longer be deceived!

11. I know that I can do all things through Christ.

12. God's gifts and His calling are irrevocable, and this means God will never take back what potential He has poured into me! These gifts are my calling in my life, and they'll be with me until the day I die, but I know it's up to me whether I decide to tap back into them again!

I took a step of faith, and God has brought me places I never dreamed possible. When God puts a dream in your heart, it may look impossible in the natural. Every voice may tell you, it will never happen, but if you believe and stay in faith, and expect good things, you can beat the odds and overcome anything! I needed to start looking where I wanted to be; to start dreaming again, and DREAM BIG DREAMS! God can resurrect any dream!

I needed to let go of my life disappointments and let go of my failures and make those doors entirely close behind me. I needed to step forward into the future that God has in store for me, knowing there's nothing I can do about past disappointments and failures. Besides, what's in front of me is more important. I've been told, that's why we have such a large front windshield and such a small rearview mirror because it's far more critical to look ahead than at the hurts and pains from the past! Nothing will keep me from the good things of God as much as living in the past. Whatever I do, I can't stay down! I must get up and knock the dust off myself, find encouragement, get up in the morning, put my shoulders back, look in the mirror, and say "I've come too far to quit now!" I can't say it is good enough, because good enough is just halfway!

I needed to understand that when I came to know Christ, I received His forgiveness. God cleaned out all my closets. He chooses not to remember my mistakes, my sins, and my failures.

My question is why don't we quit remembering them? I think it's because God doesn't want to remove some of the pain, memories, and hurt that we've caused others through our selfish actions. Why don't we quit listening to the voice of the accuser? I think because that's God wanting us to be more dependent and focused on Him!

How Can This Help You?

I listened to Worn, by Tenth Avenue North today as I was sitting filled with failure. It summed up what I was feeling and going through. "I'm tired, I'm worn; my heart is heavy from the work it takes to keep on breathing." Give this song a listen to sometime; it helped me in some of my lowest times emotionally.

It took a while, but I finally learned to stop focusing on all the negatives and to stop looking at everything I have lost and start looking at all that I have remaining! I have started believing that things are now changing for the better, not because I deserve it, but only because God loves me that much.

I read this in a Joel Osteen book:

"Remember your actions will follow your expectations! Low expectations will trap you in mediocrity; high expectations will motivate you and propel you to move forward in life. But raising your level of expectation is not a passive process. You must acquire positive thoughts of victory, thoughts of abundance, thoughts of favor, thoughts of love and hope, good, pure, and excellent thoughts!"

As a leader, I needed to refuel my mind, redevelop my abilities, and further my next career. I needed to feed my mind on a regular basis with good, pure, and compelling information. Feed my mind with positive seminars, good books, CD's, inspirational books, positive learning material, and the good old Bible! I was away from this for years, what happened to me? Was I too good to learn anymore? Was I too successful? Or just too lazy living in sin and complacency and not taking time to nourish my soul, my mind, and my body? Thank you, Lord, for shaking my tree and waking me up!

A very close friend said this to me:

"Those who might criticize your business decisions or management skills or suggest that you are nuts are simply envious. I remain in awe of your vision and your enthusiasm— and I'm proud to call you my friend. You have been good for this City, and you have been good for me!"

EVERY business decision is risky, and EVERY business has risks—EVERY DAY! But I am reminded of Milton Hershey, who failed three times before his chocolate company took off. Some time ago, I was in Orlando, and I marveled to those around me, at the commerce and growth in and around Disney. I reminded them that everyone had thought Walt Disney was flat out NUTS to invest millions in a mouse and a bunch of swamp land years ago! This "investment" was even more ridiculous considering he already had a successful TV show, movies, and a theme park in California. Why would he risk all of that? Because he had a vision and he did not live in fear of the risk—and I believe he probably shared another trait that you have! He had faith in the Lord. Keep going and keep listening to the Lord. He will guide you and all of us if we just take the time to listen.

"May my accusers perish in shame; may those who want to harm me be covered with scorn and disgrace. As for me, I will always have hope; I will praise you more and more. My mouth will tell of your righteousness deeds, of your saving

acts all day long—though I know not how to relate them all." (Psalm 71:13)

And then in verse 20, it goes on to say:

"Though you have made me see troubles, many and bitter, you will restore my life again; from the depths of the earth you will again bring me up. You will increase my honor and comfort me once more." (Psalm 71:20-21)

That is incredibly convincing!

Put actions behind your words today! I need to keep my head up and gaze upon Him! So, what do I see in my future???? Success, joy, peace, contentment, and abundant life in a relationship of faithfulness! I must never set my sights too low. Zig Ziglar says, "Shoot for the stars!" People who see their dreams come to pass are people who have some drive, even resolve with some backbone. I've always considered myself to have the courage and to not settle for just good enough, for good enough to me was still just half-assed or the cream-of-the-crap!

I think we all know the road to ruin is paved with good intentions. Don't fall into this trap, don't allow Satan to win, do not settle for mediocrity!

I only needed to focus on one bite-sized thing at a time. Set my course and have a positive attitude fill my heart with light and joy and go at it slowly. I'm not going to settle for a little love and joy, a bit of peace and contentment, or for a small helping of happiness or success! No, I'm going to reach my full potential in God and start living my life now! God created me with an incredible imagination, a very powerful image that has taken me through life's ups, and I visualize my path for success!

I recently read in another one of Joel Osteen's books, that if I write the words "Big Black Dog," you just don't see the words; your mind shows you an image of that animal, a picture that is drawn up from your mental computer memory banks. In the same way, each of us has a view of ourselves in our imaginations. That self-image is like a thermostat in our room. It sets the standard at which you will function. You will never consistently rise higher than the image you have of yourself, and you will never accomplish things that you don't see yourself performing.

When you see yourself going downhill, barely getting by, your business getting worse, your relationship getting worse, then most likely, your life will gravitate towards those adverse situations—if you allow it.

I now see myself the way I want to be—successful, motivated, happy in a relationship, not struggling. I have allowed a positive image of my life to take root with a new picture of success! I just needed to follow some simple instructions, like those of Zig Ziglar:

"We all need a daily check-up from the neck up to avoid "stinking thinking" which ultimately leads to hardening of the attitudes."

I know that I must be cautious with what I allow to come out of my mouth. Words are powerful, and they set the direction for my life. I know I've been filled with stinking thinking for a long time, but I've relearned that Scripture tells me we are to:

"...calleth those things which be not as though they were." (Romans 4:17 KJV)

And that's what I have to do with turning around my life, both business and personally, I must see it as already coming to fruition! I've done that all my life with everything I've built; I just need to do it again and always. In other words, I can't talk about the way I was, but the way I want to be, and the way I will be. That's what faith is about. We want to see it to believe it, but God says you must believe it and then you see it.

If I'm going to see these dreams come to pass, I must get my mouth moving in the right direction and use words to help me develop a new image on the inside. I am secure in the Lord, and I can do all things through Christ who strengthens me. I can fulfill my destiny. I need to call on what God has promised me. The question is what I am I saying to myself? What do I meditate on? Am I thinking positive thoughts, empowering thoughts, affirming thoughts? Or do I go around thinking negative thoughts, defeated thoughts, telling myself things like, "I'm not talented, or smart enough. I've made too many mistakes." Or worse yet, "I'm sure God is displeased with me." It's those kinds of thoughts that keep you and others from rising higher.

I can't lie in bed anymore thinking about everything that is wrong with me and my situation. I can't lie there and rehearse all my mistakes, thinking about what I can't do, or I don't have what it takes. I must shake off the negatives and remind myself that I am a child of God, and I have a bright future and that I have what it takes—I will fulfill my destiny! Get up every day and bless someone. Stop worrying about the blessings that you feel are due you! Quit feeding the bad habits—starve them into submission—and start nourishing good habits! Bad habits are easy to develop but challenging to live with. It's easy to give in to temptation and do whatever we feel. It's easy to live in bondage, feeling guilty, and condemned. Repeat after me, "I will no longer be a slave to negativity!" Be careful, negativity can be a powerful addiction.

On the other hand, good habits are difficult to develop; they require pain, hard work, and even suffering and sacrifice. Once established, good practices are easy to live with! I've heard someone say, "Habits are like gravity; they will always pull you towards them." Good habits will make your life easier, more successful, and more productive, and you won't always struggle to do the right thing when you're practicing good habits—they produce good fruit! I know that bad habits will inevitably drag me right down to the ground, hence the gravity deal, they have and always will!

Happiness does not depend on my circumstances; it depends on my will, it's a choice that I make! So, I put a smile on my face, and a good report on my lips; I will remain positive and upbeat, no matter the dilemma! It is a choice; it's all in how we train our mind. Training your mind to be hopeful, trusting, and believing for the best in any situation is an exercise worth doing! Develop a habit of happiness by just relaxing and go with the flow. Let's face it, God is in control!

Zig Ziglar says:

"If you can help someone get what they want, you'll get what you want!"

My gift is to challenge and inspire people, to encourage and give people hope; hope with relationships, hope with business, and ultimately to Honor God through all the success!

I won't allow my critics to steal my joy. My destiny will not be determined by my critics but by God. God will have the final say. Quit listening to everyone, to the naysayer, or the doomsday defense, and hold your chin up.

You cannot change your past, but your future is spotless. You can write on it what you will today; however, you need to learn to respond to the positive and the negative. Zig Ziglar talks about: "Do you respond or react? It's your choice!" Fortunately, you have far more control than you realize. For example, consider the emotion of anger. As a wise man said, "You can't stir the soup unless there's soup in the pot to stir!" Nobody can make you act mad unless there is already 'mad' in you. Angry reactions are learned behaviors, and consequently, they can be unlearned.

My response or reaction to the negative reveals what's inside of me. It exposes my heart and shows the kind of person I really am. The problem is that most people tend to react instead of responding. They tend to blame everything and everybody for the difficulties and reversals in their life. Don't do this. As Michael Jackson's song says—Look at "the man in the mirror" and make a change.

Chapter 23

LUCK: WHEN PREPAREDNESS MEETS OPPORTUNITY!

I am doing suicide sprints in the gym at my Junior High School. I hear the shrill shriek sound of that awful whistle every few seconds, as our team runs up and down the court like robots. After the suicide sprints, our coach would have us jump rope non-stop for what seemed like an eternity! I remember heading to the shower after practice and walking down the stairs from the gym to the locker room and my legs feeling like spaghetti! I now know that jumping rope builds stamina, agility, and leg strength, even hand-eye coordination and that in those days Coach Harry was making preparedness in us!

I remember the first time I heard Harry say, "Luck: when preparedness meets opportunity." I thought this quote was an original from my ninth-grade basketball coach. Many years later, I discovered that it was the ancient Roman philosopher named "Seneca," who was attributed with this phrase that I have now taught to many. Nevertheless, Harry would drill this into his nine-man basketball squad at every practice. You must understand we were the smallest Junior High school in the conference. We were undersized and without much talent, but he taught us you cannot win without heart. You must be motivated and driven to succeed at anything you attempt. But most of all, he would stress there was no luck in sports or in life; it was all about being able to take the advantage when an opportunity occurs. Hence the quote: the definition of luck is when preparedness meets opportunity!

Coach often would use professional basketball players as an example to us. He loved players from his era like Wilt "The Stilt" Chamberlain, or "Pistol Pete" Maravich, and even Bob "Houdini of the Hardwoods" Cousy. He would stress that they were ordinary guys with extraordinary drive and skills. I don't know about you, but Wilt Chamberlain and his behemoth size were extraordinary right from the get-go! Let's face it; "The Stilt" was that one extraordinary player in history to score 100 points in a single game! That is a record that will probably stand for all eternity since Kobe Bryant is the closest with 81 points, and Wilt scored 70 points or more seven times in his career. Cousy and Pistol Pete, on the other hand, were good players who mastered the game with perfect practice; not just practice, but perfect practice for hours each day! I was amazed that "Cooz" could shoot a foul shot underhanded and swoosh it practically every time. He was like a human highlight film when he would dribble right handed and then shift to a left-handed dribble without skipping a beat.

I read that "The Cooz" was cut twice from his Junior Varsity school team because he was too small and without talent. When he was 13-years-old, he fell out of a tree and broke his right arm, forcing him to learn to play with his left arm and become ambidextrous. His former coach, Lou Grummond, witnessed the ambidextrous youngster playing in the neighborhood leagues and was so impressed, he invited him back to join the team. It turned out Grummond needed a playmaking guard, and Cousy fit the bill. So, with "The Cooz," it wasn't about luck when Grummond noticed his play that day on the schoolyards. It was about Cousy being prepared when that opportunity came about!

Like I said, our Junior High School varsity basketball team was a small team. I was one of the tallest, if not the tallest player on our ninth-grade team at 5' 11". I think I weighed 145 pounds at the time. Richard, Tommy, Gary, and Ken were our forwards and guards, and all were great ball handlers and shooters, but I was always left to do the dirty work under the boards with blocking out, and of course, I was the team's center!

Coach taught us mental toughness and preparation in everything we did and most of all, to never allow our opponent to shoot the ball uncontested. The problem was that we were not an overly tall team. Attempting to block shots for us would often have the tendency for us to commit a foul. Our coach hated fouls, in his eyes; it was a free shot and free points! So, he taught us that the proper way to contest a shot is to stay on your feet facing the shooter until the shooter leaves his or her feet, then attempt to get your hand on top of the basketball as quickly as possible! At the very least, get a hand up, so it limits his vision of the basket, so he has to shoot over you. While we may not have blocked every shot, we put their shooter under a maximum amount of pressure, and coach made us practice this over and over, just like suicide sprints and jumping rope!

We played about eight or nine different teams in our conference. One group was the school across town on the south side where everyone thought they were better than us at everything including basketball and football. They were considered rich kids, better athletes, and so on. But I must tell you when we played with coach's mental toughness and preparedness each time we faced them—when the final whistle blew—and the game was over, they always knew who they played!

There were several teams from surrounding counties all around our small town; but across the river, they had guys on their team that were 6' 5" and 6' 6" and weighed 200 pounds. I remember riding the bus to the away games and our teammates talking about their school having ex-convicts on their team, which I learned later was quite an exaggeration! But, they were big and fast and had great basketball skills, and it seemed like they always won the state basketball championship.

I think every player on our team contributed to our success that year. We left it all out on the court with every game we played. It must have been luck for our team because that year we finished our 18 regular season games with 14 wins. We beat the rich kids from south of the railroad tracks both times that year, and if I must say, by pretty good point margins as well. And I think we were lucky as well to win our conference that year by beating the big teams across the river and in the county south of us. The luck had to end sooner or later. We got knocked out of championship play in the first round, but we were conference champs for only the second time in our Junior High school's history!

So, was it just luck, or was it preparedness when the opportunity arrived for our team?

There is No Such Thing as Luck— What I Meant to Say Was...

I think the difference between lucky and unlucky people is all in our perspective. I know I have seen it many times before.

Luck isn't just about being in the right place at the right time, but also about being ready for new opportunities the second they happen.

Richard Wiseman's study has shown this:

"Create your own luck by changing your perspective! Think you have no control over how lucky you are in life? Lucky people generate their personal good fortune via four basic principles!

1. They are skilled at creating and noticing chance opportunities.

2. They make lucky decisions by listening to their intuition.

3. They create self-fulfilling prophecies via positive expectations.

4. They adopt a resilient attitude that transforms bad luck into good.

Are you a lucky or unlucky person? Or, to put it more precisely, are you prepared to be lucky?"

I love what philosophers, statesman, and writers of all time say about luck. Our third President of the United States, Mr. Thomas Jefferson, said this:

"I am a great believer in luck, and I find the harder I work the more I have of it!"

I know my situation was just like what Thomas Jefferson spoke of. The harder I worked, the luckier I became. I started selling automobiles when I was 20 years old. A year or so went by, and a light went on in my head. One day as a customer was leaving the showroom, after not buying a car from me. The customer said to me, "I want to think about it, and I will give you a call." I watched that customer leave the lot, and I thought to myself, "There is a good chance I will never see or hear from that customer again in my life." I decided at that precise moment in my sales career that I was going to read every sales book, listen to every tape (they had cassette tapes in those days) that I could get my hands on. I would train myself to watch every video that was available and to attend every seminar concerning selling and closing the deal! Well, guess what? Pretty soon, I became luckier and luckier at selling. I remember the other sales guys always saying, "He has Mr. Good Up again, or he has another lay down!" These were terms in the car business for an easy sale, and believe me when I tell you, they were all easy! I learned to sell, I loved people, and I loved to help bring joy to someone's life by helping them to buy from me!

Another man, that I think was quite smooth with his words concerning luck, was Ralph Waldo Emerson. He says this about luck:

"Shallow men believe in luck or in circumstance. Strong men believe in cause and effect."

Frankly, I don't believe in luck at all, but what I do think is that God has a preconceived–predestined plan for every one of us.

"For we are His workmanship, created in Christ Jesus unto good works, which God hath beforehand ordained, that we should walk in them." (Ephesians 2:10 KJV)

"Indeed, the very hairs of your head are all numbered. Don't be afraid; you are worth more than many sparrows." (Luke 12:7)

"…And let us run with endurance the race that God has set before us." (Hebrews 12:1 NLT)

It talks about the need for self-discipline, which to me, is all related as part of the preparation process!

"Do you not know that in a race all the runners run, but only one gets the prize? Run in such a way as to get the prize." (I Corinthians 9:24)

Paul is saying put all you have into whatever you are doing!

Here's another good quote from the book, *In the Face of Danger*, by Joan Lowery Nixon:

"Life is not easy. We all have problems, even tragedies to deal with, and luck has nothing to do with it! Bad luck is only the stupid excuse for those who don't have the wit to deal with the problems of life."

HOW CAN THIS HELP YOU?

I learned that most of us tend to blame somebody else for our difficulties but keep appropriate credit for our success to ourselves. What about me? Do I respond to the negative and make it better, or do I react to the negative and make it worse? I must not waste time placing the blame but fixing the cause!

Here's something from Zig Ziglar:

"Cooperation is not getting the other fellow to do what you want. Rather it means getting him to want to do what you want! And there's a great deal of difference by the addition of this one little word want!"

Ralph Waldo Emerson said:

"What lies behind you and what lies before you pale in significance when compared to what lies within you!"

I think what I learned most from Harry that year was this: it isn't the bigger, faster, more talented team that always wins, but the team that thinks they can!

Never ever, say never! Never assume you'll just try; because sooner or later the one that will win is the one who thinks he can. One final thing; God says, "Nothing is Impossible"—in fact, the very word itself says, "I'm Possible!"

Chapter 24

CONSTRUCTIVE AVOIDANCE

I am trapped in a place called "Constructive Avoidance." I don't know how I arrived here. But I am stuck, afraid of failure, and I will do almost anything to avoid another failure in my life. I will do anything, except what I must do! I think most of us have heard the term *constructive avoidance*. One describes this situation as when we must make things happen, but we will do anything to avoid doing what we should do! We claim that we first must do this, that and the other thing before we can tackle what has to be done. While the excuses seem utterly reasonable in our mind, the result is that we just never get around to doing what we know we are supposed to do in the first place!

I sell for a living; but, it doesn't matter what a person does for his livelihood, because it can apply to any type of work or chore that you must do that takes you out of your comfort zone. Before I understood the term of *constructive avoidance*, I used to also refer to the "intrinsic and extrinsic" things in the work we are involved in that we enjoy doing and the things that we must do. While they have similarities, there is nothing in life that compares to *constructive avoidance*! There are three kinds of people! Those that watch things happen, those that make things happen, and those that don't know what happened!

Here is my dilemma *concerning constructive* avoidance. I go to work. No—I must first go to the gym, so I can lose some weight, because being physically fit also helps your mind work better. And besides, when you interact with clients you have more energy; you look and feel better, so I like staying in shape. Oh, and I must make sure I have the perfect wardrobe for my sales job; I don't want to offend someone with the way I dress. After I get my physical body back in shape, I must go and buy a new outfit or two, so I look the part—the part of success and making that lasting first impression!

I finally get to work, and my desk and work areas are a mess. I spend the day organizing my desk, my files, my cabinets, and I clean my entire office space, so I can be organized to perform the tasks that I know I must do! Now, this function takes the whole day, and frankly, I spend several days on it.

As I am arranging my office files and making everything neat and orderly, I discover that I need some extra pens, some hanging files, along with folders and identification tags to go inside of the hanging files. I will also need to purchase some other items, so I can professionally color coordinate everything that I am about to undertake. Therefore, I must to go to the office supply superstore and buy all the items that are going to make me successful and become the most organized salesperson in my office.

Several days later, my workspace is finally put together; my supplies are up to snuff, and it is now time for me to prospect. I already understand deep-down inside that if I don't sell, I don't eat! I watch everyone around me making their phone calls and prospecting, and I tell myself that, "I can easily do what they do, and I can even do it better!" So, I start by figuring out who my prospects are?

You must understand this is another challenging step and takes a lot of my time. After all, I am a perfectionist. I don't want to do things just half way. I log on to my computer, and I figure out what areas I want to prospect. Oh, by the way, who is my prospect? I must do the research finding what each of the prospects demographics include. A key to my prospecting success is finding out what each prospect needs! Now several days later, I finally have my prospect list put together, and now I can finally call my prospects!

But wait—I must figure out how I'm going to contact each prospect. I figure, instead of just cold calling a prospect, I think I want to have someone in our marketing department design a mail piece that I can first send my prospect to introduce myself. I believe that this is necessary. So, when I finally get around to calling them about a month later, they can recognize who is calling them, and what I am calling about.

I now have the mail piece finished, and I have my prospect list completed, and I want to personalize it. So, I handwrite a note on each postcard and write a personal letter to everyone, so the prospect feels warm and fuzzy when they receive my mail piece. It will make them feel like this sales guy knows me personally!

Finally, after the post office takes several more days to deliver my long awaited, direct mail piece, it is time for me to call these hot prospects! I have just one more task of looking up each phone number and making sure they are not on the "Do not call list!" I go through all the chores of looking up phone numbers. Are they on the "Do not call list" or not? After all, I don't want to call someone and offend them, do I? A few more days have gone by, and I have my prospect list put together with the appropriate phone numbers that are not on the "Do not call list!"

I know that if I am going to be a successful phone prospector, I better have a great phone script, so I don't fumble around and sound like a rookie salesperson when I'm making these money-making calls! I decide to go online and watch videos and take extensive notes from the country's best telephone prospectors. While I'm viewing these life-changing videos, I decided that I want to buy the skills book and CD system. I order all his exciting material and anxiously await my success package to arrive in the mail weeks later. In the meantime, I drive to the local book superstore and grab another one or two of those bestsellers that walk you through a step-by-step script to making millions while never leaving the office! I am intrigued by the titles: "How to Earn Millions Fast!" and "Dialing for Dollars." I make the purchases of the 250-page books that reveal the hidden secrets of America's most prosperous and most successful salespeople! These are the quick and easy ways that thousands of salespeople just like me have developed into successful professionals from the risk-free programs offered by these authors. How could this not work? I can build my confidence level and make millions with their proven prospecting methods!

Now, I'm now almost ready. I have taken day and night for weeks on end, reading and writing scripts, and have practiced them energetically with my spouse and friends alike, and now comes the time to put what I have learned into practice!

But wait it's the holiday season; who wants to be bothered by a salesperson during the holidays? I hate being worried! Everyone is under so much pressure this time of the year with the preparation and decorating for Christmas parties, and so on. I think I should wait until after the holidays, it will be better then.

The holidays come and go, now, I must deal with the winter, no one wants to go out in the cold weather and view my product this time of the year. I might as well wait until spring, when the peak of the selling season arrives and when everything starts to pop, including my business!

I'm prepared, I'm anxious, and I will start seeing my results this month! My office phone rings: I immediately think, "Could it be a prospect from one of my mailings from last fall? Oh, how I hope so. I've been working so hard at making things happen and preparing myself for a successful sales career!" "Hello?" I answer the phone excitedly. "Bill this is your sales manager, could you come down to my office as soon as you can, I need to talk to you about something." My sales manager answered. "Ah... sure, I'll be down in just a minute!" Hmmm... maybe he wants to talk to me about being an assistant sales manager, or maybe I'm going to get a promotion? As I walk to the boss's office, I'm approached by everyone in the office and hear their kind comments, "Oh, he is so nice, well dressed, handsome, and organized. He will do so well in this business!"

I knock on my manager's closed office door. A loud "Who is it?" came from inside. "Hi, Boss, it's Bill, may I come in?" "Yes, come in!" I open the door. I enter his office; he offers me a seat in front of his big mahogany desk! "Bill, I know you, and I go back a long time." "Yes, I sure do know that; we have had some good times and memories over the years, haven't we?" I replied. "Bill, this is one of the hardest things as your boss and a friend that I'll ever have to do!" "What is that?" I say with concern. "I have to fire you. I must let you go. I know you've been working hard, your advertising pieces are better than anyone's in the company, your ideas are great, and your effort is tireless, but your sales numbers are terrible! I'm under pressure from upper management to hire salespeople that will produce results *now!* I have to let you go, I'm sorry, Bill!"

AVOIDING CONSTRUCTIVE AVOIDANCE
WHAT I MEANT TO SAY WAS...

No, I didn't get fired! But, that's just what can happen with *constructive avoidance.* You put everything else in front of what you should be doing, and that is working at doing business! A.R. Bernard is quoted as saying:

"A man without a future is bound to return to his past!"

Starting today, I will strive to make a future for myself, without *constructive avoidance*! Eddie Windsor sums it up well by saying this:

"Next to hardness, you will find excuseness!"

No one ever said that sales or prospecting or *constructive avoidance* is easy! But, there can be no excuse for constructive avoidance, other than being a coward! I don't know many of us who can look at themselves in the mirror and say: "You're a coward!" What? Is that too bold or harsh? Let's face it; it is a cold fact, that most of us are afraid to pick up the telephone and call someone we have never met before or knock on a door that we have no idea what lurks behind the door. But let me tell you there is hope! Hope in knowing that the person on the other end of that phone line or the person on the other side of that door is human. They are human and no better than you are. They get up in the morning and put their pants on the same way everyone else does, and that is one leg at a time. You see fear is nothing in God's eyes: hundreds, even thousands of people have been in more dangerous situations than yours, and they did not fail!

Whatever your constructive avoidance is, it's mainly fear based. Fear of rejection, fear of failure, fear of being turned down. Why? Are you afraid of success and what success will do for you? Think of all the things you can do with success! Everyone feels worried at some point, whether it's a gnawing, anxious feeling, or a paralyzing phobia. Any change, even positive changes like marriage or a promotion, or also prospecting as I referred to, can prompt feelings of fear. The Bible offers hundreds of compelling alternatives to those voices of failure ringing through your subconscious; the sounds that are constantly reminding you repeatedly, "You can't make it; you can't do it, you will never be a success, and so on!" Click those negative voices off, tune them out, and listen to God and His positive words! I told you some time back that Satan will use his tools of defeat, rejection, and failure on you if you are weak and allow him to take advantage of you.

Here is a verse or two that helped me realize that I can overcome anything:

"These people are blemishes at your love feasts, eating with you without the slightest qualm—shepherds who feed only themselves. They are clouds without rain, blown along by the wind; autumn trees, without fruit and uprooted— twice dead!" (Jude 1:12)

John, the writer, is saying they are worthless, fear or being afraid or avoiding something will never hurt you!

God knows that people who have been trying to honor Him have been tempted with failure, defeat, rejection, and constructive avoidance, but He offers hope!

Check out I Corinthians, and see what Paul has to say:

"Be on your guard; stand firm in the faith; be courageous; be strong." (I Corinthians 16:13)

"Keep your lives free from the love of money and be content with what you have, because God has said, 'Never will I leave you; never will I forsake you.' So, we say with confidence, 'The Lord is my helper; I will not be afraid. What can man do to me?'" (Hebrews 13: 5–6)

What can they do to you? This is what I was talking about with people putting on their pants the same way you do, they can't hurt you! What? Are they going to make you fail? No, only fear and constructive avoidance can make you fail!

"Who is going to harm you if you are eager to do good? But even if you should suffer for what is right, you are blessed. 'Do not fear what they fear; do not be frightened.'" (1 Peter 3:13–14)

Check out 1 John:

"There is no fear in love. But perfect love drives out fear because fear has to do with punishment. The one who fears is not made perfect in love." (1 John 4:18)

Another from David, one of God's greatest overcomers:

"When I am afraid, I put my trust in you. In God, whose word I praise—in God I trust and am not afraid. What can mere mortals do to me?" (Psalm 56:3–4)

And finally, one of my favorite quotes from Joyce Meyers:

"Courage is fear that has said its prayers and decided to go forward anyway!"

I like that!

So, I ask you, "What type of person are you? Do you watch things happen? Or are you going through life not knowing what happened, or are you the kind of person that makes things happen?"

How Can This Help You?

It took a while for me to realize that success comes with a price: a price sometimes that many of us aren't willing to pay. Trust me when I say—once you get that confidence in you, your stride will be different than anything you ever felt before in your career! But you must overcome that fear first. You must trust your instincts and your own abilities—abilities that are God-given! No one has ever said this is easy. It isn't, but like anything, if it were easy everyone would do it. Do you believe in yourself? Then go for it and don't allow yourself into thinking you can't do it... believe me, you can do it!

Go ahead, look in the mirror and tell yourself that you can do this! Pray for God to release you from your fears and give you protection—protection for you to do what your family is depending on you to do, and that is to provide for them!

Pick up that phone, knock on that door. Say a polite, "Hello" to that customer on the other side of the counter and introduce yourself. Be bold because God tells you in His word to have faith in yourself! You are a success; you can do it!

Chapter 25

THE AWAKENING

Suddenly, I can feel a small amount of consciousness. I'm not sure, but it feels like there is water splashing around my face, neck, and mouth? I can feel water passing around me, as I'm trying to get my whereabouts. I can feel that most of my body is wet, but I don't know why. "What in the world is going on?" I think to myself. It's chilly water. I can feel my shirt, and even my pants are soaked—I think I'm lying in shallow water. "Am I lying in a creek bed?" I wonder, trying to make sense of it all. My eyes blink open and close to try and focus and to connect my mind with my surroundings.

I hear noises nearby, but I'm not sure of where they're coming from. I can faintly hear men talking. All of a sudden, I hear a voice a little clearer from the top of the bank of the creek. "Bill, are you okay? Bill, can you hear me, are you okay, Buddy?" I manage to lift my head high enough to get my face out of the tall grasses in the creek. I try to elevate my upper body to lift my torso and face from the muck and sand from the creek's edge. I look up and see my friend Mark. "Bill, what the heck happened to you? Are you okay?" I can hear the concern in his voice. "Mark, I'm not sure. I'm not even sure how the heck I got here. I can't make sense of what's going on."

Mark gets down on his knees and sticks out his arm to help me try to get up from the creek bed. "Dude, what the heck are you doing down in the creek?" Mark says with almost a chuckle—trying to make light of what could be a serious situation. "I told you, I don't know," I reply with frustration. But, things are starting to come together. I remember now that Mark and I were supposed to play golf together, but he phoned me to tell me he was running late because of a patient he had to see at the last minute.

"Geez, you're heavy, buddy, you're soaking wet!" Mark is now facing down on the ground above me, flat on his chest on the bank, extending both arms trying to grab my arms to help me up. He strains to pull me upright, as I try to get up on my knees and eventually to my feet. Four feet below Mark, I manage to crawl to the bottom of the bank. Shaken, but now standing there soaking wet, trembling from the cold water, I shake the grass, sand, and mud off my arms. In Mark's normal humorous voice, he says, "Bill, if you wanted to go swimming, don't you think you could have picked a warmer day? How did you end up in the creek anyway?" Things are finally starting to come together for me, albeit slowly, but coming along.

With Mark's help, I manage to crawl up the bank and sit down at the edge of the creek. "Here, drink something," Mark says as he hands me a bottle of water from his golf cart. "Yuck!" I yell after I rinse my mouth and spit out the first swig. I had sand residue all around my lips and inside of my mouth from the creek bed! "That was nasty, nothing like a mouthful of sand and grit, let me try this again! Oh, baby, that sure tastes good!"

"Here let me help you up. Let's sit you down in my golf cart and tell me what is going on with you." Mark puts out his hand, and I take it. Still being a little foggy, he steadies me by putting his arm around my shoulder as we move to sit in the cart.

Mark being a surgeon, albeit, a cosmetic surgeon immediately starts with the 20 questions. "How did you end up in the creek?" "I hit my tee shot into the bank of the creek, and you know how I hate to lose golf balls, so I grabbed my wedge out of my golf bag. Wait a minute?" I said. Mark then replies, "What's up?" "I remember now, I had been huffing and puffing a little for a couple of holes and even had some lightheadedness now that I think about it!" "Let's get you to the hospital. Did you have chest pain?" "Well, maybe, it wasn't exactly chest pain." "If you had chest pain from a heart attack, you would know it!" Mark continues, "Look, the heart specialist at the hospital is a good friend of mine; I'm going to call Dr. Crane and get him to meet us at the hospital right away. I want him to do an EKG and some other tests on you to see what's going on with you. If you had a heart attack, I want you to know about it right now! Do you have any shortness of breath now?" I answered him quickly, "No! Why?" "Cause, stupid, you could have had a heart attack!" "Get out of here, Mark; I didn't have a heart attack!" "Do you have any pain in your arm or any chest pain now?" "No... no pain in either!" Mark says, "Let's get you up to my car in the parking lot; I have a blood pressure cuff in my car, I want to check your blood pressure at least." "Mark," I asked, "What's a plastic surgeon doing with a blood pressure cuff in his car?" "Don't ask; it was a gift for Anna's mother that I forgot to give to her the last time she was here, so it remained in my car. Who knew I would need it today?" "Mark, I probably should have told you, but everything was happening so quickly, Dr. Miller just put me on blood pressure medicine a couple of weeks ago. I have had quite a bit of lightheadedness, but I figured it was just me getting used to the blood pressure medication." "Bill, blood pressure medicine is not something you have to get used to!" "I know that Mark, I just mean... well, it's the first time I ever had to take it."

We arrived at Mark's car, greeted with a massive stare by the cart boy, "Geez, Mr. Kolovani, are you okay? What the heck happened to you? Your outfit is all muddy, and your face and arms look like you were mud wrestling. Were you rolling around in the creek?" Mark quickly answers for me: "Yes, Rocky, that's putting it mildly, he didn't like his shot on the fifth, so he decided to take a dip... headfirst into the creek!"

Rocky and Mark help me out of the golf cart. Again, Mark jumps in and takes over the situation. "Rocky, let's seat Mr. Kolovani in the front of my car first. Then—if you don't mind—Bill's clubs and his pull cart are down by the fifth green where I found him. If you could drive my cart down there and grab his cart and clubs and throw them in his pickup that would be great!" Mark reaches in his pocket and hands Rocky a 20-dollar bill. "Thank you, Dr. Simpson, that's very generous of you!" Even though I just took a header in the creek, I hadn't lost my sense of humor. "Hey Rocky! He'll probably bill me for it anyway!" "Wow, you're a big tipper buddy, are you really going to tack that on my bill?" Mark replies, "No, that's all Anna gave me to spend today. Mark hollers at Rocky, "You might as well throw my clubs in the trunk of my car right away while you're at it!" "Yes sir, Dr. Simpson, is there anything else I can do for you?" "No, thanks Rocky, we are fine, thanks for your help!"

I sit down in Mark's plush leather passenger seat, "Nice ride, dude... Did your neighbors up on the hill make you get rid of your Suburban?" I say jokingly. "Billy, I don't work 70 hours a week and perform emergency surgery on a facelift gone bad on Christmas Eve to drive a 12-year old suburban!" "I'm just busting on you, buddy, I know you work your tail off." "You know I just pulled your behind out of the creek, you a feisty old codger!" "Feisty, yes... codger, no!" "You dragged me away from my near perfect golf game to take my blood pressure, even I want to know what it is now." Mark puts on the blood pressure cuff like he just got out of med school. "What? Did you forget how to do this?" Mark replies, "No, I've just never used one of these new high-tech cuffs, and besides the staff in my office handles all that kind of stuff. I don't think I have taken anyone's blood pressure in 10 years."

Beep... Beep... Beep... "Wow, this thing is quick; I see why they like these new BP cuffs. Bill, it's no wonder you were light-headed, your blood pressure is way low." I asked, "What's way low?" Mark responds with, "How about 102 over 59—you're a dead man walking!"

We're both sitting in the front seat of Mark's new ride. He grabs his cell phone and proceeds to call his friend Dr. Crane, at the General. Dr. Crane is a member of the golf club as well. Other than seeing him in passing occasionally, I really didn't know him. I did, however, remember he was a friend of Mark's and that he was the best heart guy in the valley. Mark explained my situation to him, and Dr. Crane instructs Mark to drive me to the General right away, and he would meet us there in 15 minutes.

The club is only about 10 minutes away from the hospital. As soon as we arrived, they were anxiously waiting at the emergency room door with a wheelchair. They immediately wheeled me to a private area in the emergency ward and instructed me to disrobe and put this little powder green gown on. A male nurse came in and helped me onto the examining table. "Mr. Kolovani, we'll need you to fill out a little paperwork, and if you don't mind, while you are doing that, I am going to clean some of the mud off you. Dr. Crain will want your skin as clean as possible with all the tests he ordered."

Dr. Crain had ordered every kind of heart test imaginable. An EKG electrocardiogram, a stress test, and two other tests including an "Echo" which I knew was an echocardiogram—a test that uses ultrasound to evaluate your heart muscle and heart valves and—finally, a CT scan.

As I'm getting prepped for all the tests, Mark must have called my wife, and she showed up as well, scared to death, and worried sick about my wellbeing! I told her all about my dip in the creek at the golf course and how Mark discovered me.

Dr. Crain performed everything. I don't remember ever having tests like this done in my life! About two hours or so later, after they were finished pinching, poking, prodding, and testing my heart, Dr. Crain says: "Zip Zero, Zilch! Other than a little low blood pressure your heart is healthy!" Dr. Crain called Dr. Miller to inquire about my blood pressure medication and changed that to a new med that had just been released. You know how the drug companies want the doctors to try all the new medications first, and free samples were excellent.

Before Dr. Crain released me, we had the opportunity for me to walk through the entire episode of me falling into the creek. He surmised it as nothing more than stress while carrying my golf bag up and down the hills. Stress from life (take it easy and don't work so hard and worry less was his remedy for that), and, finally, cut my cigar smoking back (what he meant to say was "quit"), and take off a couple of pounds off!

So, after what I thought was a near death experience, turned out to be a cleansing of my mind and soul from all the experiences that life had brought to me over the years. It allowed me to make peace with certain people—at least in my mind. But also—concerning the situations that didn't involve people—this allowed me to disengage those memories from my mind, digest and put them behind me once and for all. For the first time, I felt free from the loss and hurt of the past.

I could have never scripted a life like the one that I've had. Oh, I've had plenty of heartaches, but I think, as I look back, most of my grief was caused by careless decisions made on my part. A lot of my life was spent running from God instead of running to Him. Life has given me the most beautiful roller coaster ride imaginable; ups and downs turned upside down, rolled over, slammed straight down, and then, when you least expect it, shot up into the sky for another successful venture.

Chapter 26

ALL'S WELL THAT ENDS WELL!

I am free. Free as a bird, like an eagle soaring above all others. I know this feeling of confidence. I have had it dozens of times before in my life. My self-esteem has become elevated by my healthier feelings about my image—like an endorphin high on life. Why is it when you need self-esteem or confidence the most, that's when your self-esteem is the worst? Hello, think about that! I know from my tremendous highs in my past that a person with a good healthy family life, prosperous business, financial success, and strong faith in Christ will be a very tough cookie to beat! I've lived that. But I've also allowed myself to be deceived into thinking thoughts or making hasty decisions, or as some would call it, have bad luck. And bad luck will come your way when you make stupid business, family, and career decisions.

I have been blessed to have reversed virtually everything about my personal situation with relationships, with my children, and my business by refocusing a positive mental outlook and by paying attention to every small detail in my life. I allowed myself to be drawn away from the single most important thing or person in my life, and that's my personal relationship with Jesus Christ! The good news is I decided to change and re-invent myself before my health failed or before I died of old age and ended up in hell!

For me, I know that self-image plays a role in everything I do. William Shakespeare was quoted as saying:

"Our doubts are traitors, and make us lose the good we oft might win by fearing to attempt!"

Never, be afraid of trying to accomplish something great.

The man said to have the most wisdom in the world was King Solomon. He wrote in Proverbs:

"The godly may trip seven times, but they will get up again. But one disaster is enough to overthrow the wicked." (Proverbs 24:16)

Wow, how many times in my life have I fallen or met failure? But, you can grab your bootstraps and pick yourself up. If I could do it, anyone can do it!

My wife says, "Unfulfilled promises are monuments to nothing!" She told this to me a few years back. "NOW, you are accepting the responsibility, but that realization was not there for a long time!" At this stage in my life, the most important thing is that I have recognized it and have taken the right steps to correct it. And, still, sometimes the challenge remains for me to convince myself that I am who I say I am.

Success once again begins with my state of mind, with a definiteness of purpose. Success comes to those who become success conscious. And the same is true with failure. It happens to those who indifferently allow themselves to become failure conscious. The sole object of Napoleon Hill's book is to change ones thought patterns from failure to successful thoughts. We have the power to control our thoughts! That is a fact from the Bible, and I know it! Then why didn't I practice it? I was conditioned, that's why. Our brains become magnetized with the dominating thoughts which we hold in our minds, and, by a means which no man is familiar. These magnets attract to us the forces, the people, and the circumstances of life which harmonize with the nature of our dominating thoughts. So, that being realized, I have changed my thoughts to be more positive, as well as making my behavioral patterns to be positive.

I know I must have a desire to succeed, and for the first time in a few years, I have that desire again. I've burned all the bridges behind me. I do not want to return to the place I left. I now must win or perish! Like faith without works, wishing alone will not bring you riches; no more than eating a hamburger will make me Ronald McDonald. If you desire riches and have a state of mind, that becomes an obsession—then plan specific ways and means to acquire riches, and back up those plans with persistence, minus any thoughts of failure, that will bring riches. God has put me on this earth to use me, but I also know to be successful, He wants a right heart within me and a definiteness of purpose. I have the knowledge of what I want and a burning desire to achieve it!

Think about the real leaders of the world, who have always been men or women who have harnessed and put into practical use the intangible unseen forces of unborn opportunity, and who have converted those forces or impulses into chocolate factories, Ford automobiles, and every form of success known to man to make life more pleasant!

As Zig Ziglar says:

"Help someone get what they want, and you'll get what you want!"

To win the big stakes in today's world, you must catch the spirit of the great pioneers of the past whose dreams have given our civilization all that it has of value—the spirit which serves as the lifeblood of our own country. Practical dreamers do not quit!

It is said by Napoleon Hill: "Put your dreams across and never mind what 'they' say if you meet with temporary defeat for 'they' perhaps do not know that every failure brings with it the seed of an equivalent success!"

A burning desire to be and to do is the starting point from which the dreamer must take off. Dreams are not born of indifference, laziness, or lack of ambition. Remember many who succeed in life get off to a bad start, and pass through many heartbreaking struggles, before they arrive. I have, you may have, and many have experienced it! The turning point in the lives of those who succeed usually comes at the moment of some crisis through which they are introduced to their "other selves."

No one is ready for a thing until they believe they can acquire it, and this state of mind must be a belief, not a mere hope, or a wish! And this can happen with one little victory. All it takes is something to start the ball rolling in the right direction, and faith that removes your limitations. Faith is believing what you can't know or see. While I believe in Jesus Christ as my personal Savior, I also think that I'm going to get through any hardship that I'll face now, or in the future, but we must put action into works now!

As I examine my life at this point, I know my life matters. The critical point in this book was making a difference in someone's life, no matter how small or insignificant it may seem. I genuinely believe that I've lived my life in such a way that I've always tried to make a difference in people's lives. I even said recently that when I leave this earth, I hope people find that I left it better than I found it! So many people go through life with insignificance. I want to make a difference. I want the people to whom I sell a home, or for whom I sell a home, to feel like they received more than they paid for!

And finally, here's the bottom line! One ship sails east, and the other ship sails west, both using the same wind, it's kind of like a thermos bottle, one's hot, and one's cold, but how does it know the difference? You can decide how your life is going to be by how you set your sail! Life is 10% what happens to you and 90% how you react to it.

Some men are driven to distraction and despair by the wind of circumstance. Trouble comes; defeat, failure, discouragement, and even tragedy—people crack, and they cave in, and collapse in another direction and often end up in a circle!

It's not only the altitude of my attitude—for that comes and goes, as well—but it's how I process this information that's up to me. How is my resistance to trials? People go through similar circumstances as I have all the time and it's how they react to the situation that makes them an individual of integrity. Are they becoming seasoned, tempered, mellowed, and mature, or do they just fly off the handle and go in the direction they want, failing both sinfully and financially. Every temptation or adversity builds you into a stronger person; like burning the rubbish off the silver, the hotter it becomes, the purer the silver! The same holds true for steel. The more forging and hammering that transpires, the better the quality of steel. So, it goes with me. The wind blows for each of us in life, but it's how we adjust our sails that make the difference.

Today, don't take defeat, failure, adversity, disappointment, frustration, and mistakes as final. Set your sails on God and trust in Him. Setting your mind on the flesh is setting yourself up for failure. He'll let all the wind drive you—on course—toward your destination!

My "Get out of the pit" prayer for you is: "Your people will rebuild the ancient ruins and will raise up the age-old foundations; you will be called Repairer of Broken Walls, Restorer of Streets with Dwellings." (Isaiah 58:12)

If I've learned one thing in my amazing life, it is this: you can tell how deep-seated a man's faith is by how he reacts when he is in desperate need—that's when he'll either choose to fight or take flight!

One of my all-time favorite movies is The Natural. In the movie actress Glenn Close says this quote so well:

"I believe we have two lives; the life we learn with and the life we live with after that!"

For me, that was my life; what I said, and then, what I meant to say, was...

About the Author

Bill lives in Virginia Beach, with his wife Dr. Edna V. Baehre-Kolovani (recently retired community college president) and their Boykin Spaniel "Stogie." Bill's love for helping people has taken him from the golf course and retirement to his most recent career of real estate. His life passion is to bring joy to someone when their paths cross; whether it's providing a client with more than they expect when they buy or sell a home or just picking up a newly found friend and taking them for coffee.

In his free time, Bill still gets enjoyment from golfing; but much higher ranking in the pecking order is playing Paw-Paw to his grand girls! He loves his real estate career, but his hope is that he can make a difference in people's lives no matter how they connect. Bill's desire is to enrich someone's life through the love of Christ!

If you would like to contact Bill you can reach him on Facebook at: **whatImeanttosay or at whatImeanttosaybook.com.**